Gardening
in
New England

Also by Marion Schroeder

The Green Thumbook
The Green Thumb Directory

Gardening in New England

A RESOURCE GUIDE

Marion Schroeder

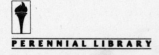

PERENNIAL LIBRARY

HARPER & ROW, PUBLISHERS, New York
Grand Rapids, Philadelphia, St. Louis, San Francisco
London, Singapore, Sydney, Tokyo, Toronto

FIRST EDITION

Designed by Alma Orenstein

Maps by Frank Ronan

Library of Congress Cataloging-in-Publication Data

Schroeder, Marion.
    Gardening in New England: a resource guide/Marion Schroeder.—1st ed.
        p.   cm.
    Includes index.
    ISBN 0-06-096433-2 (pbk.)
    1. Gardening—New England—Directories. 2. Gardening—New York (State)—Directories. 3. Nurseries (Horticulture)—New England—Directories. 4. Nurseries (Horticulture)—New York (State)—Directories. 5. Gardening equipment industry—New England—Directories. 6. Gardening equipment industry—New York (State)—Directories. I. Title.
SB450.943.U6S36   1990
635'.025'74—dc20   89-45714

90 91 92 93 94 MV/MPC 10 9 8 7 6 5 4 3 2 1

Contents

Introduction

This book is intended as a guidebook—a sort of garden atlas or travel directory—to plants, places, and people in New England and New York.

These seven states—Maine, New Hampshire, Vermont, Massachusetts, Rhode Island, Connecticut, and New York—are just a small part of the United States as a whole. (They'd all fit nicely into Arizona with room for several Rhode Islands to spare.) But they have a huge number of gardening resources—especially dedicated, enthusiastic gardeners—far out of proportion to their size.

If you're traveling through New England and New York, or new to the area, I hope this book will introduce you to many of these people and resources. Each state section features, in addition to nurseries, places to visit: arboretums, public gardens, and museums. Look for the 🌿 symbol. And for those of you who are natives of the area, perhaps it will help you discover a few people, places, and plants that you haven't known before. If so, and if this book adds to your enjoyment and interest in gardening, it will have accomplished its purpose.

Good gardening!

Some Explanations . . .

Someone once said that all sourcebooks are inevitably incomplete. That's true of this book. It's by no means a *complete* guide to garden resources in the Northeast. A number of places, for one reason or another, are not listed. However, that's not a reflection on their quality, and I hope you will understand if a favorite nursery or garden of yours is missing.

And as this is mainly a "go to" book, some well-known and well-respected mail-order companies are not included. But most of them are familiar to gardeners around the country.

Another comment on sourcebooks is that all should have a strong caveat emptor clause; so buyer, beware. I've quoted a lot of people in this book and if they say they have the best, or the biggest, or the most beautiful, well, in their enthusiasm they may be stretching things a bit. But judge for yourself, before you buy.

Personally, I think you'd have to look long and hard to find a more scrupulous and finer group than these plant people. And I think you'll agree with me after you meet them.

About Those Directions . . .

At the beginning of each state section you'll find a map that should give you a general idea of where places are located. And with a great deal of help from a lot of people, I've tried to give specific directions for finding each place.

A suggestion: Get an *individual* map of each state in which you'll be driving. State tourism offices have excellent ones; they're usually available at the "welcome centers" that you'll find on most major highways as you enter a state. (Or write in advance to the state offices listed below; there's usually no charge for a map.)

If you should get lost, try calling ahead to the place you want to go. And remember, except for New York State, the

Northeast is a relatively small, compact area. So you can't be too far out of the way.

Good luck!

State Tourism Offices

Connecticut
Department of Economic Development, 210 Washington St., Hartford, CT 06106

Maine
Maine Publicity Bureau, 97 Winthrop St., Box 23000, Hallowell, ME 04347-2300

Massachusetts
Office of Travel and Tourism, 100 Cambridge St., Boston, MA 02202

New Hampshire
Office of Vacation Travel, P.O. Box 856, Concord, NH 03301

New York
Department of Economic Development, 1 Commerce Plaza, Albany, NY 12245

Rhode Island
Department of Economic Development, 7 Jackson Walkway, Providence, RI 02903

Vermont
Travel Division, 134 State St., Montpelier, VT 05602

— Connecticut

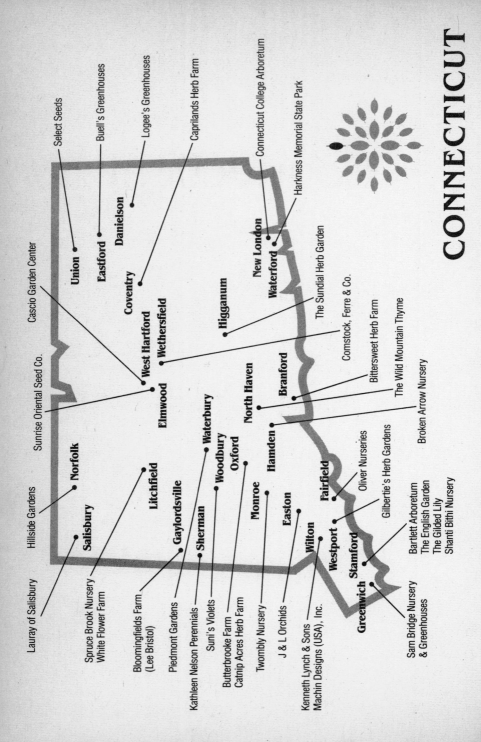

CONNECTICUT

Select Seeds

Buell's Greenhouses

Logee's Greenhouses

Caprilands Herb Farm

Connecticut College Arboretum

Harkness Memorial State Park

Union

Eastford

Danielson

Coventry

New London

Waterford

Cascio Garden Center

West Hartford

Wethersfield

Higganum

The Sundial Herb Garden

Sunrise Oriental Seed Co.

Elmwood

North Haven

Branford

Comstock, Ferre & Co.

Bittersweet Herb Farm

The Wild Mountain Thyme

Broken Arrow Nursery

Hillside Gardens

Norfolk

Salisbury

Litchfield

Gaylordsville

Waterbury

Woodbury

Oxford

Monroe

Easton

Hamden

Fairfield

Oliver Nurseries

Gilbertie's Herb Gardens

Lauray of Salisbury

Spruce Brook Nursery
White Flower Farm

Bloomingfields Farm
(Lee Bristol)

Piedmont Gardens

Kathleen Nelson Perennials

Suni's Violets

Butterbrooke Farm
Catnip Acres Herb Farm

Twombly Nursery

J & L Orchids

Sherman

Wilton

Westport

Stamford

Greenwich

Bartlett Arboretum
The English Garden
The Gilded Lily
Shanti Bithi Nursery

Sam Bridge Nursery
& Greenhouses

Kenneth Lynch & Sons
Machin Designs (USA), Inc.

Bittersweet Herb Farm
777 E. Main St.
Branford, CT 06405
(203) 488–1599

HERBS, HERBAL PRODUCTS,
DRIED FLOWERS

David and Jill Wallace, Owners

Direct retail sales; open Mon.–Sat., year-round, 10 A.M.–5 P.M., Sun., 11 A.M.–5 P.M. Also mail-order sales; free catalog.

Take exit 56 off I-95 near New Haven; northbound take a left off the exit ramp, southbound take a right; go to third traffic light (1/4 mile), and turn right; 1 mile ahead on Rte. 1 on right-hand side.

Bittersweet Herb Farm began life as a working chicken farm. But the Wallaces chased out the chickens, converted some of the buildings into studios for craftspeople, made room for an herb shop, and planted herbs and flowers for drying. They now grow 8 acres of herbs and flowers.

They sell potted herb plants in the shop from March through July and also carry a large selection of culinary herbs as well as herbs for decoration, drying, and medical purposes.

One of their specialties is herbal vinegar. Using herbs grown on the farm, they add several bushels, freshly picked, to a 45-gallon drum of distilled white vinegar. Flavors include chive blossom, dill, eleven-herb, opal basil with oregano, cilantro, parsley, sage, rosemary, and thyme. The Wallaces also have herbal mixtures for dips, fragrant oils, and potpourri.

They have a large selection of flowers for drying—statice, silver king, globe amaranth, coxcomb, strawflowers, and more. The Wallaces often sell herbs, herbal products, and dried flowers at craft fairs throughout the Northeast.

Caprilands Herb Farm
534 Silver St.
Coventry, CT 06238
(203) 742–7244

HERBS AND RELATED ITEMS

Adelma G. Simmons, Owner

3

Direct retail sales; open every day, year-round (except for some major holidays) 9 A.M.–5 P.M. Also mail-order sales; send large, self-addressed stamped envelope (SASE) for brochure.

From Hartford take I-84 east (toward Boston) to exit 59 (Rte. 384); take Rte. 384 to Rte. 44; then go east on Rte. 44 to Silver St.; turn right.

At Caprilands you'll find herb plants and seeds, many varieties of scented geraniums, garden items such as markers, sundials, sculptures, flower cutters and other garden tools, herb seasonings, fragrances, oils, potpourri, herb teas and herb jellies, dried flowers, and much, much more.

Caprilands is famous for its dried flower and herb wreaths which were introduced over thirty-five years ago. A favorite is the Advent Wreath with symbolic Christmas herbs, available in November and December. (It's recommended that you order these early.)

Among the places to visit at Caprilands are the Greenhouse Gallery, the Herb Barn, the Bouquet and Basket shop, the thirty-one different gardens, the eighteenth-century farmhouse that is open for luncheon programs and special teas and dinners, and the bookshop. The latter includes many books on herbs by Adelma Simmons, proprietor, who began Caprilands in 1929.

Garden tours and programs are presented daily and special programs are held throughout the year. Send a large SASE for a brochure listing these, or pick one up when you're at Caprilands.

Logee's Greenhouses   BEGONIAS, OTHER RARE PLANTS
141 North St.
Danielson, CT 06239
(203) 774–8083
                                      Joy Logee Martin, Owner

Direct retail sales; open every day, year-round, Mon.–Sat., 9 A.M.–4 P.M., Sun., 10 A.M.–4 P.M. Also mail-order sales; catalog $3 (refundable).

In northeastern Conn.; take exit 92 on Rte. 395; go north on Knox Ave. to Westcott Rd., then go west to Rte. 12; go north on Rte. 12 to North St.; go right (west) to greenhouses.

"Like walking into a botanical garden!" is what visitors often say when they enter Logee's. Among the hundreds of plants on display—including begonias, geraniums, cacti, gesneriads, and orchids—you'll see mature specimens of *Bougainvillea, Jasmine, Camellia, Acacia,* and *Allamanda,* many of which are over fifty years old.

Logee's can claim a number of superlatives. It's the oldest horticultural business in Connecticut in continuous operation by one family. (Joy Logee Martin's father, William D. Logee, founded the business in 1892.) It's considered one of the country's foremost mail-order greenhouses. And it has the largest begonia collection in the East. (Well over 125 varieties of rex begonias alone.)

In addition to the plants mentioned above, Logee's offers many herbs, perennials, and choice home and conservatory plants such as *Abutilon* (flowering maple, more than a dozen varieties), *Anthurium, Buddleia, Crossandra, Euphorbia, Ficus, Hedera* . . . the list goes on and on, all the way to *Westringia,* an Australian plant with tiny silver leaves topped by white flowers.

If these are too many choices for you, relax. Logee's will put together a collection for you to get you started.

Guided tours are offered for garden clubs and groups. Call for an appointment.

A don't miss!

Buell's Greenhouses, Inc. GESNERIADS
11 Weeks Rd., P.O. Box 219 MSG
Eastford, CT 06242 Albert H. Buell and
(203) 974–0623 Diantha B. Buell, Owners

Direct retail sales; open year-round, Mon.–Sat., 8 A.M.–5 P.M.; closed Sun. and major holidays. Also mail-order sales; send 25 cents plus self-addressed stamped envelope (SASE) with 45 cents postage on it for brochure.

In the northeast corner of Conn.; go 2 miles north of U.S. Rte. 44 and Conn. Rte. 198 to center of Eastford; at first full stop sign take West-ford Rd. to Weeks Rd. (just past cemetery); the greenhouses are on Weeks Rd., at the top of the hill on the left, 6/10 mile from the stop sign.

Albert H. Buell is internationally known in the horticultural world for his Buell's Hybrid Gloxinias, first introduced in 1947—the year he started his business. Since then he has had many new introductions and, as you might expect, gloxinias and their relatives are profuse in the Buell's 22,000 square feet of greenhouses.

Here's a rundown on some of the plants you'll find: *Aeschynanthus* (lipstick vine); *Boea; Columnea; Episcia; Chirita; Codonanthe; Nautilocalyx; Petrocosmea; Streptocarpus;* gesneriads with scaly rhizomes, such as *Achimenes, Kohleria,* and *Smithiantha;* gesneriads with tubers such as *Chrysothemis* and *Sinningia*—from *S. pusilla* (only 2 inches) to *S. speciosa* (from 12 to 20 inches)—the spectacular "florists gloxinia."

Not to be forgotten, of course, is what is probably the world's most popular blossoming house plant—the African violet. Buell's have about 140,000 growing in their greenhouses, representing over 800 varieties.

The greenhouses are a showplace and people are welcome to browse, hands-on, in most of the ½ acre under glass. Groups are welcome, whether they come in buses or private cars.

You'll also find growing supplies here and one of the most popular items is Buell's Miracle Soil, which comes in bags of various sizes. It is rich, composted *real* soil, same as is used in the greenhouses. Many people come to Buell's just to stock up on it.

Buell's Greenhouses are highly recommended for everyone with an interest in these plants (and also for those who aren't yet acquainted with them). Well worth a special day's trip!

J & L Orchids   ORCHIDS
20 Sherwood Rd.
Easton, CT 06612   Cordelia Head, Lucinda Winn, and
(203) 261–3772   Marguerite Webb, Partners

Direct retail sales; open Mon.–Sat., 9 A.M.–4 P.M.; closed major holidays and Christmas Eve at noon; also closed day before semiannual sales in late Jan. and late June; call ahead if planning a visit near that time. Also mail-order sales; catalog $1.

Take Merritt Pkwy. to exit 46; go north on Rte. 59 for 4 miles; turn right at the stop sign; Sherwood Rd. is the third left after stop sign.

J & L offers a wide variety of orchid plants, specializing in unusual species, miniatures, and plants that can be grown in the home. More than 2,000 plants can be found at one time in the company's greenhouse.

The partners are very active in the orchid world, exhibiting and often lecturing at shows throughout the country as well as in Canada, Europe, and Japan. They also teach courses in the spring and in fall at the New York Botanical Garden (NYBG). For dates and registration information call NYBG at (212) 220–8747.

A good time to visit J & L is during the annual summer sale, usually starting the last Saturday in June and the annual

January thaw sale, starting the last Saturday in January. Be sure
to call or write to confirm dates.

J & L orchids, started by Janet and Lee Kuhn, has been
in business for over twenty years.

Sunrise Oriental Seed Co.   ORIENTAL VEGETABLE
103 Eagle Dr.   SEEDS, BOOKS
Elmwood, CT 06110-0058
(Mailing address: P.O. Box 10058,
Elmwood, CT 06110-0058)
(203) 666–8071   Lucia Fu, Owner

    Mail-order sales only; catalog $1.

If you're looking for oriental vegetable seeds and don't find them
here (among the 150 varieties Sunrise has) Ms. Fu says they'll
make a search for them. The company has several consultants,
horticulture professors at a nearby university, who come from
China and Taiwan.

They'll also try to answer any questions regarding growing and use of the vegetables. And when you order seeds, complete information sheets, which include recipes, are sent with
many of them.

The catalog, printed in both English and Chinese, also
lists flower seeds (which, Ms. Fu says, oriental people love), and
a great many books on culture and cooking.

Oliver Nurseries   RHODODENDRONS, AZALEAS, DWARF
1159 Bronson Rd.   CONIFERS, ALPINES, PERENNIALS
Fairfield, CT 06430
(203) 259–5609   Scott S. Jamison, President

    Direct retail sales; open every day, March–May, 8 A.M.–5 P.M.;
Mon.–Sat., June–Aug., 8 A.M.–4:30 P.M.; every day, Sept.–Nov., 8 A.M.–
5 P.M.; Mon.–Fri., Dec.–Feb., 9 A.M.–4 P.M.

From Conn. Tnpk. (I-95) take exit 20 westbound (to N.Y.) or exit 21 eastbound (to New Haven). From exit 20, at the bottom of the ramp, turn right onto Bronson Rd.; the nurseries are ⁸/₁₀ mile ahead, immediately on the left after second stop sign. From exit 21, turn left at the foot of the ramp onto Mill Plain Rd., passing under turnpike; at the four-way stop, turn left again onto Sturges Rd.; bear right at first intersection, continuing on Sturges Rd. through one stop sign and across a stone bridge; at stop sign, turn right and continue ³/₁₀ mile to nursery on left.

Oliver Nurseries, with its parklike appearance and many mature display gardens, has hundreds of rock garden plants, pines, azaleas, and dwarf rhododendrons. It also offers a large number of alpines, wildflowers, and perennials—many of them not available elsewhere in New England.

Although Oliver doesn't sell by mail it puts out a catalog, which is one of the most useful around. The 132 pages fully describe plant material along with much cultural information and growing suggestions—a bargain at its $3 price. Order one or pick it up at the nurseries. The nurseries also publish a quarterly newsletter, which is very informative.

Jamison says he and the people on his staff are enthusiastic plant lovers, glad to help customers. And he adds, "Their specialties range from the propagation of alpine plants to the specifics of soil science, and from landscape design to the pruning of shade trees."

Dwarf Conifers

With the increasing popularity of dwarf conifers, many gardeners should find the following excerpts from "Dwarf and Rare Conifers," written by Joel Spingarn, a noted dwarf conifer expert, of interest.

. . . Today with smaller gardens becoming the norm, [the use of dwarf conifers] in the rock garden and landscape is certainly gaining in popularity.

. . . One can find dwarf conifers in every imaginable outline: pyramidal, fastigiate, pendulous, umbrella-like, or little congested cushions; also there are the irregular contorted forms that offer so much character.

During the cold months many of the dwarf conifers can be of considerable value in lending a cheery note to the garden. There is an enormous range of colors to choose from: deep purple and silvery blue to bronzy gold and bright yellows, some variegated with splashes of color rivaling many flowers. This group offers color and character for winter as well as summer interest.

Dwarf conifers originate in many ways. The majority of these plants occur from seed, and these forms are usually very stable and rarely revert. Another group is derived from the propagation of witches'-brooms, an abnormal condition occasionally found on a branch of an otherwise normal tree. Other dwarf forms are the result of environment, sometimes called climatic dwarfs. These plants become stunted or prostrate in their effort to survive the high altitudes and bitter cold of mountain regions. Examples of these can be found among the junipers, pines and firs.

Many dwarf conifers are quite rare; however, a number of forms can usually be found at specialty nurseries. Some grow so slowly that there is a dearth of cutting material for propagation, so collectors' demands cannot always be satisfied.

Reprinted from *Oliver Nurseries News,* Vol. 1, No. 1, by permission of Joel Spingarn and Oliver Nurseries.

Witches' Brooms?

"Witches'-brooms," as referred to by Joel Spingarn, are not the vehicles witches use to fly around on Halloween. Rather, the reference is to a dense, bushy growth, often found on conifers such as spruce, pine, and fir, caused by a parasitic fungus and mite.

The only damage they do is to make the host tree unsightly. When plants are reproduced by cuttings, the same dwarf characteristics are retained, and there is always the possibility that good dwarf specimens can be obtained from these growths.

_____

Kathleen Nelson Perennials   HARDY,
Mud Pond Rd.   LOW-MAINTENANCE
Gaylordsville, CT 06755   PERENNIALS
(203) 355–1547   Kathleen Nelson, Owner

Direct retail sales only; open Fri.–Sun., May–June, 10 A.M.–5 P.M.; also most other days, weekdays, and weekends, Apr.–Sept. "Take a chance or call in advance."

Gaylordsville is 7 miles north of New Milford, Conn.; nursery is 2 miles from Gaylordsville on Mud Pond Rd.; going north on Rte. 7 cross Gaylordsville Bridge, turn right, then make a quick left onto South Kent Rd.; go 1¹/₁₀ miles, turn right (Long Mountain Rd.), go across the railroad tracks, and turn left; take the next left (Mud Pond Rd.); the sign is on the left about ¹/₂ mile.

Kathleen Nelson says, "I became a mad gardener many years ago, starting from scratch with no knowledge and really adverse conditions (from maple trees and hardpan to deer, woodchucks, and design disasters). With lots of reading and lots of trial and error I progressed to a huge garden that, if never quite what I hoped, is pretty spectacular anyway and getting better each year. This experience enables me to provide my customers with firsthand advice on plants, conditions, and care."

Nelson sells hundreds of varieties of perennials—plants she has chosen for their beauty, their adaptability, and their low maintenance.

"I'm an advocate of low-maintenance gardening," she says, "that is, the practice of choosing plants and growing practices

that will give the maximum amount of show for the minimum
amount of work."

Her stock is varied, from simple old-fashioned favorites
to rare new plants, from tiny rock garden plants to the giant
Heracleum mantegazzianum (Queen Anne's lace, with gigantic divided leaves), from fancy hybrids to common natives. Many of
the plants are hard to find for sale elsewhere; they might be old
plants temporarily out of fashion, or wild plants, such as *Thalictrum polygamum* (meadow rue), that have gone unnoticed.

Nelson is glad to help her customers, and she designs
and installs gardens for clients. These services are expanding as
Nelson's husband has joined the business full-time to do general landscape design.

Her display gardens, which you are welcome to visit, are
around 2,000 square feet. If you'd like to see what they look
like ahead of time, find a copy of the first issue (May/June 1988)
of *Fine Gardening*. A picture of Nelson working in her garden
is on the cover, and there's a very interesting article she wrote,
along with color photos, titled "A Gardener's Progress."

Sam Bridge Nursery & Greenhouses   PERENNIALS,
437 North St.   NURSERY STOCK
Greenwich, CT 06830
(203) 869–3418   Samuel F. Bridge III, Manager

Direct retail sales only; open Mon.–Fri., 8:30 A.M.–5 P.M.

*Take Merritt Pkwy. exit 31; nursery is 2 miles south, on right-hand
side.*

Ninety percent of all the plant material sold here is grown by
the nursery. Perennials are the specialty, with more than 900
varieties offered; each season is started with over 50,000 potted
plants, one to three years old. To give you an idea of the extent
of Bridge's stock, currently 19 varieties of dianthus, more than

70 varieties of iris, dozens of sedum and sempervivum, and some 25 varieties of veronica are available.

In addition to perennials, Bridge grows about 300 varieties of annuals, plus an assortment of potted plants, hanging baskets, herbs, vegetables, vines, roses, and a number of seasonal plants. The nineteen greenhouses at the center are kept filled.

You'll also find an assortment of nursery stock, including many rare dwarf and unusual conifers. And also a selection of garden supplies—pottery, fertilizers, pesticides, peat moss, pine bark, and more. Gardeners in Greenwich should be able to find what they need at Bridge Nursery.

Broken Arrow Nursery   KALMIA (MOUNTAIN LAUREL)
13 Broken Arrow Rd.
Hamden, CT 06518   Dr. Richard and Sarah Jaynes,
(203) 288–1026   Owners

Direct retail sales; open Fri. and Sat., Apr. 1–June 15, Labor Day to Oct. 15, 8:30 A.M.–5 P.M. Also mail-order sales; send self-addressed stamped envelope (SASE) for list.

Hamden is between New Haven and Waterbury; the nursery is in the northeast corner of Hamden, just off Gaylord Mountain Rd., 2 miles from Rte. 69 in Bethany.

The Jayneses began their nursery in 1984 when Richard, wanting to expand his mountain laurel research, left the Connecticut Agricultural Experiment Station after twenty-five years of plant breeding.

The nursery, as might be expected, specialized in *Kalmia latifolia,* better known as mountain laurel, with red budded, deep pink, banded, and miniature varieties. Other plants include *Cornus kousa* (dogwood), dwarf conifers, *Halesia carolina* (Carolina Silverbell), Canadian and Carolina hemlock, hollies, Japanese maples, *Pieris, Rhododendron, Stewartia,* and *Styrax japonicus* (Japanese Snowbell). The Jayneses mention that their small plants make nice gifts, and are available for plant sales or as "favors."

The Jayneses also do commercial and residential landscaping, specializing in woodland or naturalistic plantings. In fall and winter they often give illustrated talks on domesticating mountain laurel.

Richard Jaynes is also author of *Kalmia, The Laurel Book,* which is recognized as the only complete and authoritative study of laurels. Published by the Timber Press in 1988, the book has approximately 225 pages and 146 photos (127 of them in color). This book can be obtained from Broken Arrow Nursery or from your bookseller.

One final thing: In 1947 as part of a 4-H project the Jaynes family planted their first Christmas trees. They now have 20 acres of trees, at three locations, that you can choose and cut. Call the nursery for information.

The Sundial Herb Garden   HERBS, EDUCATIONAL
Extension off Brault Hill Rd.   SERVICES
Higganum, CT 06441
(Mailing address: 59 Hidden Lake Rd.,
Higganum, CT 06441)   Ragna Tischler Goddard,
(203) 345–4290   Owner, Herbalist

Direct retail sales only; open weekends May 1–Dec. 24, 10 A.M.–5 P.M.; additional Christmas hours, every day, Nov. 1–Dec. 24, 10 A.M.–5 P.M.; open other days by appointment.

The garden is located just off Rte. 81, 3 miles south of Rte. 9 and about 10 miles north from exit 63, off Rte. I-95; turn west on Brault Hill Rd. (opposite the Partridge Market), follow it to the end, and bear right for about 1/2 mile; watch for signs and barn.

To better appreciate Sundial Herb Garden, here's some background on Ragna Tischler Goddard, owner and herbalist. She was born in Kiel, West Germany, and studied graphic design at Kiel University (where her father is professor emeritus in ecology and her grandfather was a professor of botany), then continued her studies in London.

After coming to New York in 1963 she worked as a graphic designer, then as an art director, and met her husband Tom, also a graphic designer. They moved to Connecticut in 1969 and began to restore an eighteenth-century farmhouse.

As the Goddards worked on the restoration they realized the gardens, planted in twentieth-century style, didn't fit in. So, combining her knowledge of horticulture with her background in art Ragna began to create three gardens: the Knot Garden, which duplicates gardens from sixteenth- and seventeenth-century Europe; the Main Garden, a typical eighteenth-century garden with a sundial in the center surrounded by geometric walkways; and the Topiary Garden; the gardens are carefully composed and form an outdoor room with the house.

The herb shop is located in an eighteenth-century restored barn and offers a variety of herb plants during the growing season, along with garden ornaments, many herbal items, and an extensive selection of books.

The barn also is the site of the tearoom where tea is served Sunday afternoons at 3 P.M., June through September; here herb tea and dessert are accompanied by herb talks and a guided tour of the gardens. Three times during the season high teas, which include sandwiches and pâtés, are scheduled. The teas are very popular, and advance reservations are required.

Visitors are always welcome to see the gardens and herb shop free of charge during open hours.

Preceding Christmas, the Sundial Herb Shop is open every day with a variety of gift items: mulling spices, dried herbs and flowers for arrangements, gourmet items, herb and spice wreaths, garlic braids—even frankincense and myrrh.

In addition to all these activities, Goddard offers lectures and programs on herbs at the Sundial and at other locations.

Visit.

Spruce Brook Nursery
Rte. 118
Litchfield, CT 06759
(203) 482–5229

NURSERY STOCK,
LANDSCAPING SERVICES

David Johnson, President

Direct retail sales; open every day, Apr.–July, 9 A.M.–5 P.M.; Thurs.–Sat., July–Sept., 9 A.M.–5 P.M.; Thurs.–Sun., Sept.–Nov., 9 A.M.– 5 P.M.; every day, Nov.–Dec., 9 A.M.–5 P.M.

From I-84, go north on Rte. 8 to exit 42; then travel west on Rte. 118 for 1½ miles.

Founded in 1947 by Arthur Johnson, Spruce Book Nursery specializes in rare and unusual trees, shrubs, and broad-leaved evergreens, with many in landscape sizes. The nursery offers complete landscape services. It specializes in naturalizing with emphasis on the New England style of landscaping—conservative in nature with New England plantings in borders.

The Living Screen Center features a variety of conifers in large sizes—up to 20 feet, which result in almost "instant" landscaping. (Smaller sizes of all varieties are available for the "do-it-yourself" gardener.)

In addition to the nursery areas, there are permanent display borders, which help gardeners visualize final results.

White Flower Farm
Rte. 63
Litchfield, CT 06759
(203) 567–0801

PERENNIALS, SHRUBS, BULBS

Eliot Wadsworth II, President

Direct retail sales; open from 2nd Fri. in April through last Sunday in Oct., Mon.–Fri., 10 A.M.–5 P.M., Sat., Sun., and holidays, 9 A.M.–5:30 P.M. Also mail-order sales; three catalogs $5 (refundable).

On Rte. 63, 3 miles south of Litchfield.

The retail store at the farm is usually kept fully stocked, and it has numerous signs to guide you to what you're interested in—perennials, flowering shrubs, shade plants, or whatever. But it might be a good idea to invest $5 in the White Flower Farm catalogs *before* you visit the farm. The catalogs (three per year) with their color photos, detailed descriptions, and cultural advice are often valued as reference books.

With your spring copy in hand you'll better be able to identify what you see in the display gardens. And you'll see a lot; the farm has some 800 varieties of perennials, 300 varieties of bulbs, and many, many shrubs.

The farm grows the perennials and shrubs it sells and backs up everything with a very solid guarantee. Your money is cheerfully refunded up to a year for any purchase that was properly cared for but failed to grow.

The White Flower Farm was started by William B. Harris in 1950 and was sold to Wadsworth in 1977. Wadsworth, who has a Harvard Business School degree, became disenchanted with banking and thought it would be a lot more interesting to run a nursery. He still thinks so, apparently, and under his management the farm has been greatly expanded and maintains a reputation of quality and high standards in the nursery business.

You should enjoy a visit there and you'll find an informed staff that's glad to help.

And, who knows, when you're browsing around you might even meet that genial sage of the horticultural world, Amos Pettingill.

Twombly Nursery   NURSERY STOCK, LANDSCAPING
163 Barn Hill Rd.
Monroe, CT 06468   Kenneth and Priscilla Twombly,
(203) 261–2133   Owners

Direct retail sales; open Mon.–Sat., Mar.–May and Sept.–Nov., 8 A.M.–5 P.M., Sun., 9 A.M.–5 P.M., closed Sun. June–Aug.; winter, by appointment. Also mail-order sales; free catalog.

Take exit 27A from I-95 or exit 49 from Merritt Pkwy. to Rte. 25; take Rte. 25 north to Rte. 111 and then to Rte. 110; turn left on Barn Hill Rd.

The nursery, which was begun in 1963, covers about 14 acres, and until recently, was wholesale only. It has a wide range of plant material, specializing in dwarf conifers, rock garden plants, rare and unusual shrubs, and small trees. Services include general landscaping with tree and lawn care.

Because the nursery was a wholesale operation, it is large enough to offer quantity discounts to retail customers.

Connecticut College Arboretum
Connecticut College Arboretum
Williams St.
New London, CT 06320
(203) 447–7700

Open every day, dawn to dusk.

From I-95 northbound take exit 83; follow Rte. 32 north about ¼ mile to campus on left; cross campus to arboretum gate. From I-95 southbound cross Golden Star Memorial Bridge over Thames River; take exit 84N to Rte. 32 and college entrance, on left; cross campus to the arboretum.

The arboretum covers 425 acres in the city of New London and the town of Waterford, and although its basic purpose is to support the botany, zoology, and other departments of Connecticut College, it is open to the public.

There are more than 300 types of cultivated woody plants. Plant collections include native azaleas, mountain laurels, conifers, and wildflowers. About 200 acres of forests and wetlands are permanently preserved as a refuge for native plants and wildlife.

You can pick up brochures of self-guided tours and a guide to campus trees in a small box just inside the main entrance on Williams Street. Other low-cost bulletins are available at the Arboretum Office, 206 New Long Hall and in the college bookshop.

Hillside Gardens   PERENNIALS, MANY UNCOMMON
515 Litchfield Rd. (Rte. 272)
Norfolk, CT 06058
(Mailing address: P.O. Box 614,   Frederick and
Norfolk, CT 06058)   Mary Ann McGourty,
(203) 542–5345   Co-Owners

Direct retail sales only; open every day except holidays, May–Sept., 9 A.M.–5 P.M.

From the center of Norfolk (in west central Conn.), go 2⁴/₁₀ miles south on Litchfield Rd. (Rte. 272); the nursery is on the east side of the road; the sign is at driveway.

Go to Hillside Gardens and talk to one of the McGourtys. Take Fred, for example. Fred McGourty was an editor of the well-known Brooklyn Botanic Garden Handbook series for fifteen years; his articles on gardening have appeared in *The New York Times, Esquire, Yankee, The Royal Horticultural Society Journal,* and he writes regularly for *American Horticulturist.* He was awarded the prestigious Gunlogson Medal for his contributions to home gardening and also received awards from the New York Botanical Garden and the Massachusetts Horticultural Society. Among the books he has written are *Perennials: How to Select, Grow and*

Enjoy Them (HP Books, 1985), which has already become a classic, and *The Perennial Gardener* (Houghton Mifflin, 1989).

Then there's Mary Ann. Mary Ann McGourty has written articles for the *American Horticulturist* and wrote the Brooklyn Botanic Garden Handbooks, *Perennials and Their Uses* and *Gardening Under Lights*. She's the major contributor and editor of *Taylor's Guide to Ground Covers, Vines and Grasses* (Houghton Mifflin, 1987) and has served as horticultural consultant for several book publishers. She also lectures and teaches short courses and workshops on gardening subjects.

So what this adds up to is that at Hillside Gardens you're truly in the hands of experts.

The McGourtys developed extensive display gardens at their home in Norfolk, emphasizing pleasing arrangements of colors, textures, and foliage. The business was started, in part, because people who saw the gardens asked for sources for the many uncommon perennials.

The criteria for their plants are that they must be hardy enough to thrive and survive in New England winters and also to hold up in the often hot summers; they should be disease and insect resistant, easy to propagate, need no staking, and last but not least, have attractive foliage and blooms.

All plants must first pass the test period in their gardens before being offered for sale—and only 20 percent of their trial plants make it to market.

You're not apt to find any hybrid tea roses at Hillside Gardens (in New England, Fred McGourty says, roses are expensive annuals) but here are some choice plants you may find.

Aruncus aethusifolius (Korean goatsbeard), 8 inches high, similar to a miniature astilbe, white flowers followed by cinnamon seed capsules, grows in shade.

Miscanthus sinensis 'Silver Feather,' which has 8-foot-tall stalks with elegant plumes of grayish flowers in late summer; leaves turn tawny in winter and look lovely against evergreens.

Athyrium goeringianum 'Pictum,' Japanese painted fern, with silver, green, and maroon markings; the aristocrat of hardy ferns.

Sedum 'Vera Jameson,' handsome gray-maroon foliage with pink flowers on 7-inch stems, choice and uncommon in the United States.

The McGourtys also design and install perennial borders. The borders in their display gardens are beautiful examples of what they can do—and visitors are welcome.

The Wild Mountain Thyme   IRIS
(Formerly Wethersfield Iris Garden)
486 Skiff St.
North Haven, CT 06473   Dr. Richard Kiyomoto,
(203) 248–8718   Owner

Display garden; call ahead. Mail-order sales; free catalog.

Take Merritt Pkwy. (Rte. 15) to Whitney Ave. exit; Skiff St. is off Whitney Ave.

Fred Gadd founded Wethersfield Iris Garden in 1948 and, due to age he says, he has turned the stock over to Richard Kiyomoto. But Gadd will continue hybridizing—which is his big interest. He has been crossing pure aril with tall bearded and standard dwarf iris, producing arilmeds. One of these introductions, 'Sizzle,' won the William Mohr award, the highest award for this type of iris.

"Start with good strong growing stock that grows well in New England," says Gadd, "and I do believe iris will grow well anywhere in the country."

Among iris available at The Wild Mountain Thyme are tall bearded iris, arilbred iris and all median iris, Japanese iris, and a selection of rare and unusual varieties. These all are on view at the display garden.

Bed and Breakfast on a Seed Farm

Tom Butterworth of Butterbrooke Farm in Oxford, Connecticut, produces open-pollinated, chemically untreated seeds of plants suited to short growing seasons. He also runs the Butterbrooke Farm Seed Co-op for which, among other things, he publishes a quarterly newsletter. He also writes garden guides, such as *How to Save Seed from Your Own Garden Produce* and *How to Build and Use a Root Cellar*. He sells a two-hour videotape, narrated at Butterbrooke Farm, that gives step-by-step instructions for growing healthy veggies. He also runs a mail-order business.

And—not the least of his activities—he operates the Butterbrooke Farm Bed and Breakfast where guests have a chance to learn firsthand about the activities of seed farm operation. Amenities include a bedroom with double bed and phone, an adjoining private sitting room with television, and a private bath in a restored 1711 colonial saltbox house in the historic Quaker Farms section of the town of Oxford. Included in the stay is a continental breakfast with fresh picked strawberries, raspberries, or melons in season from the farm's gardens.

For more information write or call Butterworth, 78 Barry Rd., Oxford, CT 06483; (203) 888–2000.

Butterworth also sells those seeds by mail, with personalized, same-day order fulfillment. Send him a large self-addressed stamped envelope (SASE) for a free catalog.

Catnip Acres Herb Farm　　　　　　HERBS, EVERLASTING
67 Christian St.　　　　　　　　　　　　　　　FLOWERS
Oxford, CT 06483
(203) 888–5649　　　　　　　　　　　Dean Pailler, Owner

　　Direct retail sales; open Tues.–Sun., Apr. 1–Christmas Eve, 10 A.M.–5 P.M.; closed holidays. Mail-order sales of seeds, dried flowers, and books; send self-addressed stamped envelope (SASE) for list or $2 for two-year catalog subscription.

no longer mail order

now run by Jean P.

*Take I-84 to exit 15, go south 4½ miles on Rte. 67—or take Rte. 8 to
exit 22, go north 4 miles on Rte. 67—to Christian St.; then go north
½ mile on Christian St. to Catnip Acres.*

"We began growing catnip," says Dean Pailler, "for one of our
cats who was a finalist in an 'All-American Glamor Kitty' contest
. . . and it just went from there. We now grow a dozen varieties of catnip alone."

Pailler grew that first catnip back in the 1970s, and today
Catnip Acres has gained national recognition for the scope of
its herb varieties. Over 400 different herb plants are featured
in the display gardens, including more than 100 types of scented-
leaf geranium—the largest collection in the United States.

The farm also has an extensive list of everlasting flowers,
with many varieties available by separate color, for example,
eight colors of globe amaranth, eight annual statice colors, seven
larkspur colors, and so on.

Catnip Acres is located in a peaceful New England country setting, and visitors are invited to wander through the gardens, savor the scents and colors in the herb barn, and look
through the greenhouse where each variety has an informative
card giving Latin and common names, cultural habits, and uses
(almost a herbal education in itself).

In addition to plants and seeds, you'll find rosemary, bay
laurel, sweet myrtle, lemon verbena, scented-leaf geranium, and
other herbs trained as topiaries.

Lauray of Salisbury   GESNERIADS, BEGONIAS,
Undermountain Rd., Rte. 41   ORCHIDS, CACTI, SUCCULENTS
Salisbury, CT 06068
(203) 435–2263   Judith Becker, Owner

Direct retail sales; open every day, 10 A.M.–5 P.M. (in rare cases,
closed, best to call ahead). Also mail-order sales; catalog $2.

On Rte. 41 (Undermountain Rd.), 3½ miles north of the junction of Rte. 41 and Rte. 44 in Salisbury.

Lauray's has one of the largest selections of gesneriads in New England, and if you're looking for that rare, unusual, or hard-to-find plant chances are good that you'll find it here.

For example, Lauray has some forty varieties of *Aeschynanthus*, more than sixty varieties of *Columnea*—plus numerous *Boea, Episcia, Streptocarpus, Achimenes, Nautilocalyx,* and *Sinningia*—and many more.

Gesneriad fanciers will recognize many breeders' names: Lyon, Worley, Schwarz, Arndt, and Katzenberger, to mention a few.

Gesneriads, however, are just a part of Lauray's offerings. There are some 200 varieties of *Begonia*, many *Hoya, Peperomi,* cacti, and other succulents and an extensive selection of orchids—*Oncidium, Phalaenopsis, Cattleya, Dendrobium*—with many varieties of each.

In the summer months there is big display of hanging plants, including fuchsias and tuberous begonias.

Lauray's participates in a number of flower shows and at those times selection of plants at the greenhouse may be limited. The big shows are the Hartford Flower Show, the New York Flower Show, and the New York Orchid Show. These take place during February, March, and April.

The company was founded in 1960 by Laura and Ray Becker. Their daughter, Judith, is now the owner.

Bloomingfields Farm (Lee Bristol)   DAYLILIES
Rte. 55
Sherman, CT 06784
(Mailing address: Gaylordsville, CT 06755)   Lee Bristol,
(203) 354–6951   Owner/Operator

Direct retail sales; nursery open Wed.–Sun., June 1–Aug. 31, 9 A.M.–4 P.M. Also mail-order sales; free catalog.

On Rte. 55, 1¼ miles east of Rte. 7 and 4¼ miles east of Rte. 22 (in N.Y.).

Lee Bristol has been growing daylilies for more than twenty years and he has over 700 varieties in his nursery with about 200 cultivars available for sale each year.

Plants range in size from 12 to 42 inches. Colors include yellow and gold shades, pale yellow, apricot and tangerine, melon and peach, pink and rose, lavender and purple, red, and white. Bloom season in Zone 5 (western Connecticut) can extend from late May to early October by planting varieties that are "extra early," "very early," "early," "early midseason," "midseason," "late midseason," "late," "very late," and "rebloomers."

Daylilies can be planted any time from April through November, says Bristol, although fall plantings should be mulched to prevent winter frost heaving.

He avoids using pesticides. Instead he relies on rotenone, a plant extract, along with the "good bugs," lady beetles, and green lacewings. Plants are mulched with wood chips and sawdust from sawmills and fertilized with manure from sheep, horses, and chickens. All in all, he says, daylilies are very easy plants to raise.

Bristol has an extensive trial garden to ensure new and superior offerings every year. He provides personal treatment to all his customers and, he says, an "unconditional guarantee of satisfaction."

The Daylily Popularity Poll

Every year the American Hemerocallis Society has its members vote on their favorite daylily. Here are the results of a recent poll of members in Region 4 (Connecticut, Maine, Massachusetts, New Hampshire, New York, Rhode Island, and Vermont):

1. Stella de Oro
2. Ruffled Apricot

3. Fairy Tale Pink
4. Joan Senior
5. Betty Woods

How were daylilies rated nationwide? These were the top ten in a poll taken that same year:

1. Fairy Tale Pink (24 inches high, 5½-inch pink bloom)
2. Becky Lynn (20 inches high, 6¾-inch rose bloom)
3. Joan Senior (25 inches high, 6-inch near white bloom)
4. Brocaded Gown (26 inches high, 6-inch lemon-cream bloom)
5. Ruffled Apricot (28 inches high, 7-inch apricot bloom)
6. Betty Woods (26 inches high, 5½-inch Chinese yellow double bloom)
7. Martha Adams (19 inches high, 6¾-inch pink bloom)
8. Stella de Oro (11 inches high, 2¾-inch gold bloom)
9. Golden Scroll (19 inches high, 5½-inch tangerine bloom)
10. Wynnson (24 inches high, 4½-inch light yellow bloom)

Notice that the five favorites from the New England–New York region are among the top ten across the country. These daylilies should thrive in a Northeast garden, and they should be beauties.

Bartlett Arboretum

University of Connecticut
151 Brookdale Rd.
Stamford, CT 06903-4199
(203) 322–6971

Open every day, 8:30 A.M.–sunset. Office open Mon.–Fri., except holidays, 8:30 A.M.–4 P.M.

Take exit 35 off Merritt Pkwy; go 1⁶/₁₀ miles north on Rte. 137 (High Ridge Rd.); turn left on Brookdale Rd. and follow the signs.

The 63-acre arboretum, part of the plant science department of the University of Connecticut, has collections of dwarf coni-

fers, rhododendrons and azaleas, wildflowers, and small flowering trees. Ecology trails and a swamp walk are laid out in the
natural woodlands surrounding the gardens.

A great many courses are offered at the arboretum, both
credit and noncredit. Some examples of one-day programs are
"French Intensive Raised Bed Vegetable Gardening," "Con-
sumers Guide to Garden Centers," "Perennial Personalities: Their
Colors, Shapes, and Textures," and "Bulb Forcing Workshop."
Numerous guided walks are held every weekend and an extensive horticultural library and a display greenhouse are open to
the public.

Two special annual events are "Winterbloom" (mid-February) and the May plant sale (mid-May).

For information about specific dates and information
about other courses call or write to the arboretum.

The English Garden, Inc.   GARDEN STRUCTURES
652 Glenbrook Rd.
Stamford, CT 06906
(203) 348–3048   David Kettlewell, President

Direct retail sales; showroom open Mon.–Fri., year-round, 10
A.M.–4 P.M.; weekend hours—depending on demand—during spring
and summer months; call first. Also mail-order sales; color brochure
$6.

*Take Merritt Pkwy. exit 36 to Rte. 106 or Conn. Tnpk. exit 9 to Rte.
106.*

The English Garden sells pavilions, covered garden seats, planters, bird tables, dove cotes, Gothic porches, trellises, and arbors.
All products are manufactured in England and are traditional
in design, Victorian in look, and very well made.

"Sophisticated, ornamental, yet very functional garden
structures," says Kettlewell.

The English Garden was originally part of Machin Designs (USA), in Wilton, Connecticut, but was purchased by Kettlewell when Machin decided to concentrate on conservatories.

The Gilded Lily   DAYLILIES
495 Westover Rd.
Stamford, CT 06902
(203) 348–8886   Lynne Rosenthal, Owner

Direct retail sales, by appointment only, Apr. 1–Oct. 31. Also mail-order sales; send want list.

From Merritt Pkwy. take exit 33, then go west to Westover Rd. and south to The Gilded Lily. From Rte. I-95 take exit 6, then go north on West Ave., bear left past the golf course to Westover Rd.; go north to the gardens.

"Daylilies," says Lynne Rosenthal, "are the ultimate carefree perennial. Depending on the culture, they can bloom from May through October."

Rosenthal has been growing and selling daylilies since 1970 and now has over 30,000 in her gardens. These represent just about all daylily colors, she says, and is the widest selection in Fairfield County. And they're reasonably priced; most are under $10.

In her display gardens, you can see daylilies growing under widely differing conditions: in sun and shade and in moist and dry soil. You can also see them naturalized and growing in combinations with conifers, other perennials, herbs, and vegetables.

Rosenthal has impressive credentials. She is a Junior Exhibition Judge for the American Hemerocallis Society; a recipient of the Certificate of Achievement from the Federated Garden Clubs of Connecticut for hybridizing daylilies; and a member of the Speakers Bureau of the New York Botanical

Garden, the Garden Club of America, Zone 11, and the Federated Garden Clubs of Connecticut. She also has a Master Gardener Certificate from the University of Connecticut.

In addition to giving lectures, Rosenthal has periodic workshops in her garden. One of her lecture topics is "edible flowers." And if you'd like to try this firsthand, she has buds and blossoms for sale—to eat.

Please Don't Eat the Daylilies!

Your daylilies may be an endangered species if there's a Chinese food epicure around. Dried daylily buds, known as *gum-jum* or "golden needles" have been a cash crop for Chinese farmers for hundreds of years. When they're dried, the buds—about 4 inches long and ⅛ inch wide—can be stored indefinitely. After they have been reconstituted by soaking in water, they add a delicate, musky flavor to soups, stews, or stir-fried dishes. Another tasty daylily snack is open flowers dipped in egg batter and deep-fried to a golden brown.

One caution: If you use daylilies for food, make sure they've never come in contact with toxic pesticides.

Shanti Bithi Nursery   BONSAI
3047 High Ridge Rd.
Stamford, CT 06903
(203) 329–0768   Jerome Rocherolle, Proprietor

Direct retail sales, open Mon.–Sat., 9 A.M.–5 P.M., Sun., 9 A.M.–4 P.M. Also mail-order sales; catalog $3.

Take exit 35 off Merritt Pkwy.; turn left and go 5 miles north on High Ridge (Rte. 137); the nursery is on the right just before the N.Y. state line.

"Shanti Bithi means 'Path of peace,' " says Rocherolle. "It's a name given to our nursery by Sri Chinmoy, Director of Peace Meditations at the United Nations."

Shanti Bithi has been importing bonsai since 1974 and today has what is one of the largest, if not *the* largest collection in North America. Selections range from *Ilex crenata* (Japanese holly), *Myrtus communis* (myrtle), and *Picea abies* (Norway spruce)—which you can take home for as little as $25 or $30—to a specimen *Buxus microphylla* 'Kingsville' (littleleaf boxwood), for which the going price is upward of $4,000. (If you drive it home, drive carefully!)

But for the true enjoyment of bonsai, create your own with a starter plant—there are plenty to select from at Shanti Bithi along with other needs such as tools, turntables, potting soil, and books to guide and inspire you.

Visitors are always welcome at the nursery, says Rocherolle, and he also has numerous lectures and courses on bonsai. Call or write for details.

Select Seeds   OLD-FASHIONED FLOWERS
81 Stickney Hill Rd.
Union, CT 06076
(203) 684–5655   **Marilyn Barlow, Proprietress**

Direct retail sales; Sat. only, call ahead (Apr. 1–May 30 for plant sales). Also mail-order sales (seeds); catalog $1.50. (Does not take phone orders.)

Take exit 73 off I-84, go west on 190 toward Stafford Springs; Stickney Hill Rd. is second right; go to old cape on right after *intersection with Brown Rd.*

"The old-fashioned 'pleasure garden,' " says Barlow, "brimming with flowers in a profusion of colors and forms, and scenting the air with unforgettable fragrances, is experiencing a welcome revival."

Select Seeds is a small home-based business, which grew out of Marilyn Barlow's desire to recreate a period flower garden to complement her restored 1835 home. She used the Old Sturbridge Village research library and its collection of nineteenth-century gardening books and catalogs and then searched for flowers throughout Europe and the United States.

Barlow now has over 100 varieties, many rarities, carefully selected for fine cutting flowers and heady fragrances. Her collection includes many native plants and flowering herbs. Some examples include *Baptisia australis,* false indigo, dating back to 1758; *Saponaria ocymoides,* basil-leaved soapwort, with pink flowers and very attractive when trailing over rocks and walls (from 1768); and *Thalictrum aquilegifolium,* meadow rue or feathered columbine, rose and white fluffy flowers, which was grown at least as far back as 1720.

Among Barlow's customers are Old Sturbridge Village, the Mount Vernon Ladies' Association, and the Thomas Jefferson Center for Historic Plants.

Plants of many varieties are available in April and May. Dates are included with those plants with a relatively recent garden history; others, not dated, are in most cases plants with a very long garden history—going back to Gerard's *Herball or Historie of Plants, 1597.*

Barlow has a display garden in the planning stages where you will be able to see plants in bloom. This should be of great interest to anyone planning a period garden.

Piedmont Gardens   HOSTAS, FERNS
517-533 Piedmont St.
Waterbury, CT 06706
(203) 754–8534   Joseph Payne, Owner

Direct retail sales; call ahead. Also mail-order sales; catalog 50 cents.

From Rte. 8 through Waterbury take exit 29, travel on Baldwin St. to Pearl Lake Rd., then to Piedmont, turn left on Piedmont. From Rte. 84 north take exit 24 to Harpers Ferry Rd. to Piedmont St., turn right on Piedmont.

"We feel that hostas are a must in all landscape gardening," says Joseph Payne. "They are relatively trouble free, neat, attractive, good for those shady spots, economical, and demand little or no maintenance for many years."

Joseph Payne's father and uncle, Philip and Henry Payne, grew hostas for pleasure and started the small business that Joseph Payne now operates. The Paynes were long-time members of the American Hosta Society and the New England Hosta Society. Among their many originations is 'Piedmont Gold,' which received the highest award at the 1978 Hosta Society Convention—outstanding hosta of the year.

If you're not familiar with hostas, you may be pleasantly surprised at the variety of sizes and colors, such as green, gold, lake blue, and yellow, with flowers in lavender and white. Payne has more than fifty varieties growing in his garden and he invites interested gardeners to come and browse. Best time to reach him, he says, is before 9 A.M. or in the evening. And he has a number of hosta originations that you can dig on your own for as little as $1 per division.

Harkness Memorial State Park
275 Great Neck Rd. (Rte. 213)
Waterford, CT 06385
(203) 443–5725

Grounds open every day, 8 A.M.–sunset; buildings open every day, from Memorial Day through Labor Day, 10 A.M.–5 P.M. Admission fee charged; lower on weekdays.

Take exit 74 on I-95 to Rte. 1 to Rte. 213. Park entrance is on Rte. 213.

This 234-acre estate, including its forty-two-room mansion, was a summer home for the Edward. S. Harkness family and was bequeathed to the people of Connecticut. It's located on Goshen Point near the confluence of the Thames River and Long Island Sound. Among the areas of interest are the Italian Garden, the Oriental Garden, the Rock Garden, and the greenhouses. Almost half of the estate is set aside for use by the handicapped and has twenty-three overnight cottages housing handicapped individuals and their counselors.

Cascio Garden Center
GARDEN CENTER, NURSERY

1600 Albany Ave. (Rte. 44)
West Hartford, CT 06117
(203) 236–5487

Kurt Fromhez, Vice President

Direct retail sales only; open Mon.–Sat., year-round, 9 A.M.–6 P.M., Sun., 9 A.M.–5 P.M.

On Rte. 44, ¼ mile west of the intersection of N. Main and Albany (Rte. 44).

Cascio Garden Center includes a garden store; garden furniture (top-quality wood and wicker); nursery stock; annuals and perennials; aquatic plants; pottery; baskets; a 3,000-square-foot greenhouse featuring exotics such as bromeliads, orchids, and bonsai; and a very large selection of bird feeders. It also offers garden design and landscaping services. There are many display beds at the center and an aquatic pond surrounded by an ornamental grass display. The facility is state of the art with video presentations, drip irrigation throughout, and a computerized inventory system.

"But mostly," says Fromherz, "we're a group of people who love plants, love to watch things grow, and love to share what we know with anyone who comes to visit."

Gilbertie's Herb Gardens, Inc.   HERB PLANTS, HERBAL
Sylvan La.   PRODUCTS
Westport, CT 06880
(203) 227–4175   Sal Gilbertie, President

Direct retail sales; open Mon.–Sat., 8:30 A.M.–5 P.M.

From Rte. 95 north take Westport exit 17; go left 1 mile on Riverside Ave.; turn left on Sylvan at Sunoco station.

Sal Gilbertie's grandfather, father, and uncles were wholesale cut-flower growers, and Gilbertie has fond memories of working as a young boy in the packing room, growing up with the fragrances of rose, carnation, lavender, sweet pea, lily of the valley, and freesia. Later the family diversified into potted plants and herbs; the demand for herbs increased so much that in 1973 Gilbertie went exclusively into the herb business.

Today Gilbertie's greenhouse has hundreds of varieties of potted herbs to satisfy whatever interests customers may have—cooking, fragrance, decorative, medicinal, or historical—or all of these. To make things easier, plants are arranged alphabetically, from aloe vera on the left as you enter to yarrow, on the far right. Labels identify plants and offer advice on growing conditions and suggested uses.

In addition to plants, Gilbertie sells numerous herbal products. And, due partly, no doubt, to Gilbertie's fond memories of cut flowers—with the emphasis on fragrance. This includes potpourri that is 100 percent botanical; pure, natural oils with floral, herbal, or spice scents; and herbal scents for misting. In the shop, you can find brochures filled with ideas for using these scents.

Comstock, Ferre & Co. VEGETABLE, FLOWER, HERB,
263 Main St.   WILDFLOWER SEEDS
Wethersfield, CT 06109-0125
(Mailing address: Box 125,
Wethersfield, CT 06109-0125)   Richard Willard,
(203) 529–3319   General Manager

Direct retail sales; open Mon.–Sat., 10 A.M.–6 P.M., Sun., 12 M.–5 P.M. Also mail-order sales; free catalog.

Take exit 26 from I-91, or take Rte. 175 from the west, to Main St., Wethersfield; the shops are across the street from the church with the white steeple (visible from the interstate), in Wethersfield's historic district.

Since its founding in 1820 by James Lockwood Belden and its purchase by William Comstock and Henry Ferre (pronounced ferry) in 1845, Comstock, Ferre & Co. has been a respected name in the seed business.

"We are well known for our responsible gardening information," says Willard. "We're not a chrome-and-glass outfit, but a down-to-earth, helpful group of people."

Comstock, Ferre now sells over 850 varieties of vegetable, flower, and herb seeds, with new ones added each year after being tested in trial gardens.

The company also has two All-America Selections (AAS) trial gardens where new plant varieties are grown and evaluated by judges known for their expertise. Mrs. Corinne Willard, President of Comstock, Ferre, and Richard Willard serve as judges for these gardens—the only AAS trial gardens in New England for both vegetables and flowers.

In Comstock, Ferre's collection of historic buildings in Wethersfield you can visit six shops. You'll find antique seed bins along with seeds and garden supplies in the Garden Center and Seed Store; there's also the Flower and Herb Store, the

Country Kitchen, the Christmas Attic, the Curtain and Home Shop, and the Greenhouse and Nursery.

Two annual events to which you're invited are an open house and field day in early August each year and the annual craft fair, the first Saturday in October, that features up to seventy-five juried crafters. Write or call for more information.

Kenneth Lynch & Sons, Inc.   GARDEN ORNAMENTS
P.O. Box 488
84 Danbury Rd.
Wilton, CT 06897
(203) 762–8363   Timothy A. Lynch, President

Direct retail sales; open Mon.–Fri., 8:30 A.M.–5 P.M. Also mail-order sales; see prices on catalogs below.

Take Merritt Pkwy. to exit 39; go north on Rte. 7 to Wilton.

Looking for garden ornaments? Maybe benches or fountains or weather vanes or sundials or statuary or figures or Japanese lanterns on wrought-iron gates or topiary forms in the shape of a peacock? Not here? You're looking for something else? No problem. Kenneth Lynch & Sons can execute your custom design.

As a starter you might order a copy of the company's catalog, *Book of Garden Ornaments.* Ordering number is 2076 and price is $8, postpaid. Other, more specialized, catalogs include *Weather Vanes, Benches, Sundials and Spheres,* and *Lighting Fixtures.* Each is $4, postpaid.

On second thought, it might be just as easy to go right to the shop in Wilton.

Joseph Kenneth Lynch, for whom the company is named, started out as a blacksmith, later worked in a metal-working shop, and eventually managed to start a shop of his own. One of his early projects was repair work on the Statue of Liberty, which had been badly damaged when a U.S. munitions ship exploded off Black Tom, New Jersey. This led to other commissions—at the New York World's Fairs, the steeple of the Old North Church in Boston, the eagles on the Chrysler Building, and the Pegasus figures for the *Reader's Digest* headquarters in Pleasantville, New York.

Back to garden ornaments. Send for the catalogs and/or go to Wilton. You'll find what you want.

Machin Designs (USA), Inc.   CONSERVATORIES
557 Danbury Rd.
Wilton, CT 06897   Miranda Kettlewell,
(203) 834–9566   Executive Vice President

Direct retail sales; open Mon.–Fri., 9 A.M.–5 P.M.; also by appointment. Mail-order sales; catalog $10.

Take I-95, or Merritt Pkwy., to Rte. 7 north; continue north on Rte. 7 for about 9 miles; the building is on the left.

Machin Designs (USA) is a subsidiary of a British company well known for its distinctive conservatories—"reminiscent of the graceful and romantic structures of previous centuries." The U.S. branch of Machin has added imaginative design and efficient construction systems.

Each conservatory is custom designed from a number of options. For example, a wood-aluminum or all-aluminum building; a choice of lengths, widths, heights, and roof styles; free standing or interfacing with existing structure; and various architectural details.

Basically, a conservatory is a greenhouse, and Machin's will provide a most elegant home for your plants.

Suni's Violets   AFRICAN VIOLETS, OTHER
208 Great Hollow Rd., Dept. MS   GESNERIADS, BEGONIAS
Woodbury, CT 06798
(203) 266–0315   Suni Roveto, Owner

Direct retail sales; open by appointment and at open houses (see below). No mail order at present.

Call or write for directions when making appointment.

"African violets are a challenge!" says Suni Roveto. "That's what makes their beauty so rewarding."

Roveto has an extensive collection of unusual African violets with speckled, striped, streaked, and bicolor flowers and variegated foliage in gold, cream, white, and pink—miniatures, trailers, and large growers with flowers up to *3 inches* across. She offers her own hybrids as well as those of many other well-known hybridizers. She also has a number of other hard-to-find houseplants, gesneriads, and begonias, which grow under conditions similar to African violets.

Roveto's background and knowledge of African violets has made her a popular lecturer. She is also an author and contributing editor to *The Gesneriad Saintpaulia News.*

An excellent time to see Roveto's plants is at the open houses she holds four times a year. If you write to her, she will put you on a mailing list for these events.

Maine

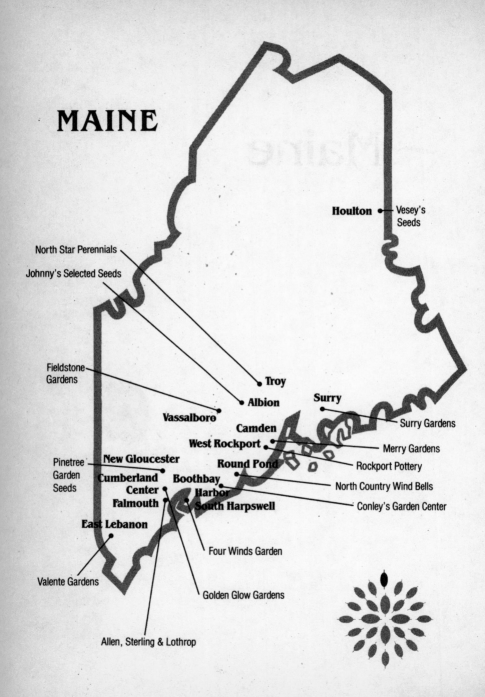

MAINE

Houlton • — Vesey's
Seeds

North Star Perennials

Johnny's Selected Seeds

Fieldstone
Gardens

• Troy
• Albion
Vassalboro •
Camden •
West Rockport •
New Gloucester
Round Pond •
Pinetree
Garden
Seeds
Cumberland
Center
Falmouth
Boothbay
Harbor
South Harpswell

East Lebanon

Surry •
Surry Gardens

Merry Gardens
Rockport Pottery
North Country Wind Bells
Conley's Garden Center

Valente Gardens

Four Winds Garden

Golden Glow Gardens

Allen, Sterling & Lothrop

Johnny's Selected Seeds
310 Foss Hill Rd.
Albion, ME 04910
(207) 437-9294

VEGETABLE AND FLOWER
SEEDS

Rob Johnston, President

Direct retail sales; shop open Mon.–Sat., Apr. 1–June 30, 8 A.M.–4:30 P.M. Mail-order sales; write for free catalog. All-America trial gardens, seed farm, and vegetable trial gardens open Mon.–Fri., July–Aug., 8:30 A.M.–4:30 P.M., for self-guided tours.

From Waterville take Rte. 137 east to Garland Rd.; go north on Garland Rd., about 3½ miles north, to Albion-Winslow Rd.; then go 4½ miles east on Albion-Winslow Rd. to Foss Hill Rd., go north on Foss Hill Rd., about ⅓ mile, to Johnny's.

When Rob Johnston started Johnny's in 1973 he said, "Our concentration is on basic food plants—thing that gardeners can really sink their teeth into . . . we are interested in providing folks with seeds for real food—not plants to impress neighbors, or varieties that will fit neatly into a packing crate."

Now, many years later, Johnny's continues as a support for home gardeners and local producers of quality and has also expanded to larger growers as well. "But we never forget," adds Johnston, "that in addition to the need for productivity, the food will be eaten and should be enjoyable and nourishing."

At the farm, use of chemical pesticides is avoided whenever possible, by composting, cover crops, and other organic techniques. With several exceptions, seeds are untreated. (Treated seed is noted.) Crops are tested in the northern climate of Albion and so many short-season plants are available.

Johnny's also manages a year-round research program for the development and screening of new food and ornamental plants. Unusual in the seed industry, the farm is used for its own seed production, supplementing dozens of producers worldwide, and operated with minimal chemicals.

The company's seed list ranges from alfalfa to zucchini,

41

with many uncommon varieties—such as old-fashioned, open
pollinated sweet corn; the European vegetable zefa fino, a fen-
nel variety; and scorzonera, a black salsify.

Incidentally, Johnny's is not named for founder and owner
Rob Johnston, but for Johnny Appleseed, aka John Chapman,
who traveled around the country sowing apple seeds.

Conley's Garden Center   WILDFLOWERS, OTHER NATIVE
145 Townsend Ave.   PLANTS, GARDEN CENTER
Boothbay Harbor, ME 04538
(207) 633–5020   Jane Conley, Vice-President

Direct retail sales; open every day, year-round, 8 A.M.–5 P.M.;
closed Sun., Jan.–Mar. Also mail-order sales of wildflowers and ferns;
catalog $1.50.

*From Rte. 1, between Bath and Damariscotta, take Rte. 27 south ap-
proximately 11 miles; Conley's is on the north side of Rte. 27; a large
sign is in front.*

Conley's, founded in 1939, is a very complete garden center,
with trees and other nursery stock, perennials, bedding plants,
vegetable plants, greenhouse plants, and a large line of gardening supplies—with many relatively hard-to-find items; also many
books and other garden publications and health foods. Conley's
provides landscaping services as well.

One of Conley's specialties is native plants—ferns, vines,
and wildflowers. Its stock includes many varieties of native bulbs
(painted trillium and yellow trout lily), native orchids (pink lady-
slipper), groundcovers and vines (trailing arbutus and shinleaf),
ferns (ostrich fern and mountain wood fern), and native perennials (shooting star, wild geranium, butter-and-eggs, and wood
merrybells). A selection of wildflowers in pots is available from
late spring to late fall.

Merry Gardens
Mechanic St.
Camden, ME 04843
(Mailing address, P.O. Box 595,
Camden, ME 04843)
(207) 263–9064; (207) 263–2121

GERANIUMS, BEGONIAS,
MANY OTHER FLOWERING
AND FOLIAGE PLANTS

Mary Ellen and
Ervin Ross, Owners

Direct retail sales. Open Mon.–Sat., year-round, 9 A.M.–4 P.M.
Also mail-order sales; catalog $1.

From Rte. 1 in center of town go south to Rte. 90; then go west on Rte. 90; ½ mile beyond intersection with Rte. 17 turn left (at Rockport Diner) and continue 2½ miles to Merry Gardens.

Merry Gardens specializes in plants that are not generally sold in garden centers and florists shops including more than 150 types of ivy, 100 varieties of herbs, dozens of scented-leaf geraniums, miniature and dwarf geraniums, fuchsias, old-fashioned begonias, and cacti and succulents. You'll find many other unusual flowering and foliage plants, such as *Sagina subulata* (Scotch moss), a hardy ground cover that is pretty as a pot plant with tiny, white star flowers, and *Acalypha heterophylla*, a dwarf plant with skeletal foliage in multicolor.

The three 100-foot greenhouses are filled with many more plants. If you can't make up your mind it might be simpler to buy one of the special collections. Merry Gardens has some suggestions: ten flowering plants, ten foliage plants, a geranium collection, an herb collection, or a collection of terrarium plants.

Gift items (great gifts for yourself) are available year-round and include live herb wreaths, with fifteen to twenty different rooted herb cuttings planted in a moss ring, a rosemary wreath topiary, and tabletop topiaries of miniature ivy in shapes such as a duck, cat, poodle, teddy bear, and squirrel.

Workshops and plant sales are held throughout the year. Call or write for dates.

Mary Ellen and Ervin Ross, a husband and wife team, founded Merry Gardens in 1946. The Rosses are also founders of Merryspring, a 66-acre horticultural park on the Maine coast near Camden. This ambitious project now includes an arboretum, a woodland garden, an herb garden, and a lily garden. Visit it when you're in the vicinity. For a brochure, write to Merryspring, P.O. Box 893, Camden, ME 04843, or get information about it when you're at Merry Gardens.

Golden Glow Gardens

115 Sligo Rd. (North Yarmouth)
Cumberland Center, ME 04021
(207) 846–9289

**LOW-MAINTENANCE
PERENNIALS**
David C. Chase,
Owner/Operator

Direct retail sales; open Tues.–Sun., mid-Apr.–Nov., 9 A.M.–5 P.M. Some mail-order sales; write for catalog.

From Rte. 95 or Rte. 1, between Portland and Brunswick, go northwest on Rte. 115 (Main St.) in Yarmouth, to Sligo Rd.; the gardens are located on Sligo Rd., 1½ miles north of the intersection with Main St., in North Yarmouth; follow the signs.

David Chase and his wife, June, started growing perennials about a dozen years ago as a hobby and in 1980 began their business. Two years later, after David retired from the U.S. Department of Agriculture Soil Conservation Service, the business really took off. The Chases specialize in low-maintenance perennials, including daylilies, heather, herbs, ferns, wildflowers, ground covers, hostas, clematis, herbaceous and tree peonies, and lilies.

They both believe in being "totally honest and forthright about the plants we sell—if there's a knock against them we say so, i.e., weedy, short lived, slow to perform, etc."

The Golden Glow Gardens catalog is very informative, giving botanical and common names of plants along with much cultural advice. It might be a good idea to send for a copy in advance of your visit.

Extensive display gardens help customers decide what they want and how to do it. The Chases are glad to work with landscapers and gardeners in designing gardens and supplying them with material.

They frequently give slide talks on perennials to garden clubs and other groups at a very reasonable cost—good to keep in mind when you're looking for programs.

Finally, Golden Glow serves as an official display garden of the American Hemerocallis Society and the American Peony Society.

Valente Gardens   DAYLILIES, IRIS, PERENNIALS
R.F.D. 2, Box 234
East Lebanon, ME 04027
(207) 457–2076   Ron and Cindy Valente, Owners

Direct retail sales; open Sat.–Sun., May 1–Sept., 10 A.M.–6 P.M. (During daylily bloom period [July] also open Thurs. and Fri.) Mail-order sales of daylilies and iris; send 45 cents in stamps for catalog.

Take Rte. 95 north in New Hampshire to Spaulding Tnpk.; continue on the Tnpk. to Rochester, N.H.; take Rte. 202 east to East Lebanon, Maine; turn right at Little River Rd. and go 3 miles to fork; take a left at the fork, then the first left (Dingham Rd.); Valente Gardens is the second place on left.

Ron and Cindy Valente began Valente Gardens in 1984 and sell daylilies (350 named cultivars), Siberian and Japanese iris, plus about 100 assorted perennials. Visitors get personal attention from Ron or Cindy.

The Valentes also design and install gardens as well as maintain them. They treat garden design in a personal manner, with input and approval of the client, and each design fits into and enhances the personal environment of the customer. Plants grown are only those that can take the demanding climate of Maine without winter mulch, are disease and pest resistant, require no staking, and are long lived.

As Ron Valente says, "Only those plants that can handle the 'real world' are sold."

The Valentes also conduct garden tours for clubs or other groups interested in daylilies during the season, July 10 to August 15.

When in Maine: Pick Blueberries . . . Shop at a Farmers' Market . . . Go to a Country Fair

Blueberries, raspberries, strawberries—Maine grown and fresh picked—can be yours if you have a little time and know where to go to "pick your own."

Or shop for organically grown vegetables, fresh flowers, dried herbs, honey and maple syrup, and home-canned jams and jellies at one of Maine's many farmers' markets.

Spend an afternoon at a Maine agricultural fair, where you'll see Maine's finest—from draft horses to potatoes—and get a close view of rural life.

Write or call the Maine Department of Agriculture, Station 28, Augusta, ME 04333; (207) 289–3491. Ask for one or all of these leaflets that they've prepared: "Pick Your Own Maine Berries," "Maine's Farmers' Markets," and "Maine Agricultural Fairs."

Allen, Sterling & Lothrop   SEEDS, GARDEN SUPPLIES
191 U.S. Rte. 1
Falmouth, ME 04105   Shirley Brannigan,
(207) 781–4142   General Manager

Direct retail sales; store open Mon.–Sat., 8 A.M.–5:30 P.M.; closed major holidays. Also mail-order sales (seeds); catalog $1.

On Rte. 1 between Portland and Yarmouth.

Founded in 1911 by Mr. Allen, Mr. Sterling, and Mr. Lothrop, Allen, Sterling & Lothrop (A. S. & L.) has been providing gardeners and farmers with seeds and supplies ever since. The company packages its own seeds—which tend to do well in this northeastern part of the country. Most A. S. & L. employees have gardened for years and are storehouses of garden knowledge, which they gladly share with customers.

Along with seeds, the store has lawn, garden, and greenhouse supplies; potting soils; bird food, feeders, and houses; garden tools and equipment; and organic gardening needs. It also has a good stock of baskets and basket-making supplies and chair-caning supplies, including prewoven caning. And last, but not least, bean pots and everything you need for canning your crops and making jellies, including stoneware crocks, up to 10-gallon size, for pickling and sauerkraut.

Pinetree Garden Seeds   GARDEN SEEDS, GARDEN
New Gloucester, ME 04260   SUPPLIES
(207) 926–3400   Richard Meiners, Owner

Direct retail sales; open Mon.–Fri., Apr. 1–Nov. 15, 9 A.M.–5 P.M. (in May and early June open every day). Also mail-order sales; free catalog.

From exit 11 on Maine Tnpk. go 5½ miles north on Rte. 100; from exit 12 on Maine Tnpk. go 5 miles south on Rte. 100.

Emphasis at Pinetree has been on the home gardener since its beginnings in 1979. You'll find a very broad selection of seeds there, and they're reasonably priced. The number of seeds in a packet is less than in most commercial packets, but it's usually plenty for a home gardener. And because of the lower prices you can try more varieties.

Pinetree has more than 600 varieties of vegetable and flower seeds and also spring and fall bulbs and perennials. Of the seeds, only about ten varieties are treated, because they were available only in this form.

The retail store has tools, watering devices, kitchen needs, organic fertilizers, soil conditioners, plant foods, season extenders, weather monitors, and some intriguing gadgets—among them is a garden tool that has been used in the Orient for centuries that's great for digging potatoes, a nitpicker for pricking out seedlings and transplanting small plants, and "terror eyes balls" from Japan, shaped like beach balls with six reflective eyes that terrorize all sorts of garden predators. Pinetree also has some 350 garden books, many of which are sold at a discount.

When you're there be sure to walk through the trial gardens, which are all around the property. You're free to visit on weekends, too, as everything is well marked.

North Country Wind Bells

WIND BELLS, GARDEN ORNAMENTS

Box 127
Round Pond, ME 04564
(207) 677-2224

James L. Davidson, Owner

Direct retail sales (mainly at shows). Also mail-order sales; write for free brochure.

From Rte. 1 take Rte. 32 south about 12 miles to Round Pond.

Through hours of listening to tapes that he recorded of the Boothbay Harbor, Bar Harbor, and Pemaquid harbor bells, Davidson was able to duplicate their haunting sounds in handcrafted steel. He also makes authentic-sounding pasture bells.

North Country Wind Bells, crafted by Jim and May Davidson, are guaranteed to rust—but only to the point of beauty. The bells are made of a premium grade of steel that, when exposed to the elements, turns a rich earthy color that blends with nature. Rusting also enhances the tone of the bells.

Other handcrafted steel products available include plant holders and boot scrapers. And one not to be missed—which Davidson says really works—is the Maine Scare Cat. It will stand guard over your gardens and berry patches and scare the daylights out of birds, squirrels, and other garden raiders.

While the Davidsons don't encourage retail sales at their shop in Round Pond (visiting interrupts production), if people find them, they'll be happy to sell. You'll also find their bells at garden shows throughout the Northeast.

Four Winds Garden   DAYLILIES
R.F.D. 1, Rte. 123
South Harpswell, ME 04079
(Mailing address: P.O. Box 141,
South Harpswell, ME 04079)
(207) 833–6620   Howard Brooks, Owner

Direct retail sales; open every day, June–Oct., daylight hours; call ahead to confirm. Also mail-order sales; free list.

In Brunswick take Rte. 123 south for about 13 miles; continue through West Harpswell; go past the small white building with a sign that reads Centennial Hall 1876; the nursery is the second house on left; a Four Winds Garden sign is at the entrance.

Howard Brooks, owner of Four Winds Garden, took over the daylily breeding lines of Dr. Currier McEwen in 1976 and now offers his own hybridized tetraploid daylilies. He sells only his own introductions rather than introductions of other hybridizers.

Brooks works with all the various types of bloom shape and form, such as spider, double, small, and large flowered and colors from almost white to yellow, orange, brown, pink, red, and purple. He aims for vigorous plants that don't need mulching or protection to survive and will grow in place for four or five years without having to be lifted and divided.

Brooks believes strongly in the therapeutic value of gardening and worked as a Horticultural Therapist at the New York University Medical Center. This was the first time horticultural activities were used in a medically oriented structured way in treating physically handicapped patients of all ages.

"People who do not know the modern daylily," says Brooks, "are missing a great deal of beauty and pleasure. They are a whole new exciting and beautiful flower. Not only are they quite easily grown, but they are easy to hybridize so you can create new varieties of your own. It makes an ideal hobby, and gardening, of course, is one of the most beneficial of exercises, not only from a physical viewpoint but because it also relieves tensions and helps solve or ease emotional problems."

Surry Gardens   PERENNIALS, DWARF CONIFERS,
Rte. 172   LANDSCAPE DESIGN
Surry, ME 04684
(Mailing address: P.O. Box 145,
Surry, ME 04684)
(207) 667–4493   James M. Dickinson, Owner

Direct retail sales; open Mon.–Sat., year-round, 8 A.M.–5 P.M., Sun., 10 A.M.–4 P.M. Also mail-order sales; write for list.

Take Rte. I-95 to Augusta or Rte. 1 to Belfast; then take Rte. 3 to Ellsworth, then Rte. 172 to Surry; the gardens are on Rte. 172 just beyond Surry.

James M. Dickinson, who founded Surry Gardens, started out in 1978 with a homemade, wood-heated greenhouse. He now has five 96-foot greenhouses and 3 acres of nursery.

Surry Gardens has many unusual perennials and several hundred varieties of bedding plants with a number of uncommon annuals; it also has trees, shrubs, and dwarf conifers.

Dickinson and his staff of professional designers and draftspeople do a great deal of landscape design and installation, working with customers' design needs and cost guidelines.

North Star Perennials   OLD-FASHIONED PERENNIALS,
Barker Rd.   PLANT
Troy, ME 04987   AND SEED SEARCH
(Mailing address: Box 2310, R.R. 1,
Troy, ME 04987)
(207) 948–2401   Sandy Olson, Proprietor

Direct retail sales; open every day, May 1–June 30, 8:30 A.M.–5 P.M. Wed.–Sun., July 1–Sept. 15, 8:30 A.M.–5 P.M. Mail-order sales planned; write for list. Send self-addressed stamped envelope (SASE) for information about plant and seed search.

Take Rte. 139, just north of Waterville, east to Rte. 9; go east on Rte. 9, past Unity, then go about 6 miles more, east to Barker Rd., turn left; North Star is 2½ miles ahead on Barker Rd. From Bangor, take Rte. 9; go 2 miles past Dixmont Corners, and go right on Barker Rd.

North Star perennials was founded because owner Sandy Olson was fascinated with old-fashioned plants that exist, for the most part, outside standard commercial offerings. The focus of the nursery is on heirloom plants, primarily herbs, perennials, and vines. She also has basket willows, dye plants, medicinal herbs, and fragrant flowers. A few gems date back to Chaucer's time, and some are plants that grew in Thomas Jefferson's gardens. Along with these, she has a collection of species clematis and a variety of honeysuckles.

Olson also operates North Star Seed and Plant Search, which locates sources for unusual perennials, trees, shrubs, fruits,

vegetables, herbs, and wildflowers from around the world. For
information about this service, write to North Star and enclose
a business-size SASE.

Fieldstone Gardens   PERENNIALS
620 Quaker La.
Vassalboro, ME 04989–9713
(207) 923–3836   Steven D. Jones, President

Direct retail sales; open every day, Apr. 1–June 30, 9 A.M.–5
P.M.; closed Mon., July 1–Nov. 20. Also mail-order; catalog $1.50 (re-
fundable).

*On Rte. 201, exactly 10 miles north of Augusta or 8 miles south of
Waterville, turn east at a state Department of Transportation sign;
follow signs from there.*

Fieldstone Gardens is a family-owned business, begun in 1980
by Steve, Carleton, and Maetta Jones, who say they have the
widest range of perennials in Maine (some 1,150 varieties). All
plants are hardy in Zone 4/5.

Customers are free to roam through 4 acres of perennial
beds and shade gardens in a hilly setting—with a background
of stone walls, fruit trees, and meadows—while they inspect and
choose plants. The Joneses and their staff are always on hand
to answer questions.

In addition to perennials there are seedlings of annuals
and vegetables in season and many garden accessories such as
tools, pottery, books, soil conditioners, hand-carved granite
birdbaths, and sundials.

A plant list, available for $1.50, which is refunded on
first order, gives detailed planting and cultural advice. Flowering season is also indicated—with blooming dates reflecting the
Maine location.

As some plants are in limited supply, Jones recommends

you call first if you have your heart set on a particular variety of plant.

Workshops are offered at Fieldstone from time to time and Jones is available for giving talks on garden subjects to groups. Write or call for details.

Rockport Pottery   BONSAI AND IKEBANA CONTAINERS,
Box 1200, Vinal Rd.   GARDEN ACCESSORIES
West Rockport, ME 04865
(207) 236–8923   Richard Robertson, Potter

Direct retail sales; open Mon.–Sat., 9 A.M.–5 P.M. Also mail-order sales; write for price list. (Majority of sales are wholesale.)

Go north on Rte. 295 to Rte. 1; then go north on Rte. 1 to Rte. 90, travel north on Rte. 90 to Rte. 17; take the first right and then take the first right again; go 1 mile to the sign.

Richard Robertson makes bonsai and ikebana containers, Japanese garden lanterns, planters, fountains, and tea ware. For bonsai that deserves the best, his specialty is custom-made containers, one-of-a-kind pieces, up to 15 gallons in capacity.

Robertson knows his art. He studied in Japan for two years, has a degree in Fine Arts from Goddard College, and did graduate work in Philadelphia. He's been potting for over twenty-five years.

Vesey's Seeds, Ltd.   VEGETABLE AND FLOWER SEEDS,
York Rd.   SHORT SEASON VARIETIES
York, Prince Edward Island
Canada C0A 1P0
(U.S. mailing address:
P.O. Box 9000, Houlton, ME 04730-0829)   B. E. Simpson,
(902) 892–1048 (P.E.I.)   President

Direct retail sales in York; open Mon.–Fri., in spring, 8 A.M.–8 P.M.; Sat., 8 A.M.–5 P.M.; Mon.–Fri., remainder of year, 8 A.M.–5 P.M. Also mail-order sales; free catalog. (Use Maine address for mail order.)

On York Rd., 5 miles east of Charlottetown, Prince Edward Island (P.E.I.).

Vesey's, founded in 1939, specializes in short-season varieties. It has a large line of vegetable and flower seeds as well as various gardening aids. Every seed offered has been grown in trial gardens in P.E.I. for two or three years to make sure that it will perform in short-season areas.

In addition to a store, Vesey's has trial gardens on P.E.I. that you can visit. (P.E.I. is also the home of Anne of Green Gables and the Prince Edward Island National Park.)

Massachusetts

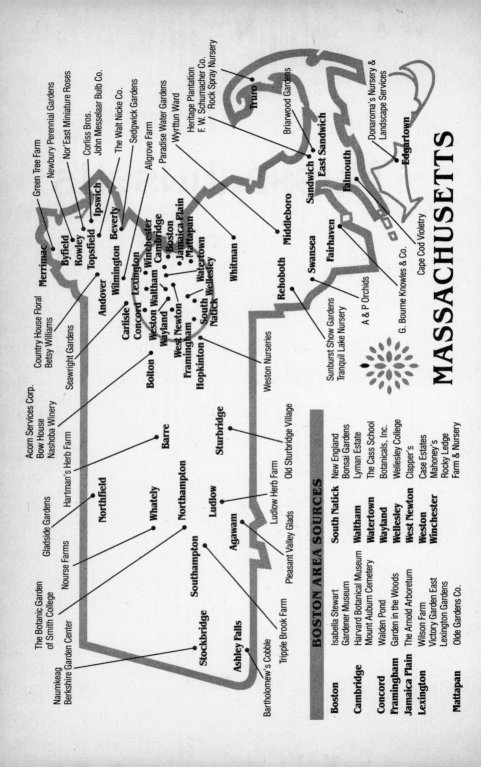

MASSACHUSETTS

Naumkeag
Berkshire Garden Center

The Botanic Garden
of Smith College

Green Tree Farm
Newbury Perennial Gardens
Corliss Bros.
Nor'East Miniature Roses
John Messelaar Bulb Co.
The Walt Nicke Co.
Sedgwick Gardens

Acorn Services Corp.
Bow House
Nashoba Winery

Country House Floral
Betsy Williams

Allgrove Farm
Paradise Water Gardens
Wyrttun Ward
Heritage Plantation
F. W. Schumacher Co.
Rock Spray Nursery

Briarwood Gardens

Donaroma's Nursery &
Landscape Services

Cape Cod Violetry

G. Bourne Knowles & Co.

A & P Orchids

Sunburst Show Gardens
Tranquil Lake Nursery

Weston Nurseries

Gladside Gardens
Hartman's Herb Farm
Seawright Gardens

Nourse Farms

Ludlow Herb Farm
Old Sturbridge Village

Pleasant Valley Glads

Bartholomew's Cobble
Tripple Brook Farm

Truro
Sandwich
East Sandwich
Falmouth
Edgartown
Middleboro
Swansea
Fairhaven
Rehoboth
Whitman
Merrimac
Byfield
Rowley
Ipswich
Topsfield
Beverly
Andover
Wilmington
Winchester
Cambridge
Boston
Jamaica Plain
Mattapan
Watertown
Lexington
Waltham
Weston
Wellesley
South Natick
Carlisle
Concord
Wayland
West Newton
Framingham
Hopkinton
Bolton
Barre
Sturbridge
Northfield
Whately
Northampton
Ludlow
Agawam
Southampton
Stockbridge
Ashley Falls

BOSTON AREA SOURCES

Boston	Isabella Stewart Gardener Museum	
Cambridge	Harvard Botanical Museum Mount Auburn Cemetery	
Concord	Walden Pond	
Framingham	Garden in the Woods	
Jamaica Plain	The Arnold Arboretum	
Lexington	Wilson Farm Victory Garden East Lexington Gardens	
Mattapan	Olde Gardens Co.	
South Natick	New England Bonsai Gardens Lyman Estate	
Waltham	The Cass School	
Watertown	Botanicals, Inc.	
Wayland	Wellesley College	
Wellesley	Clapper's	
West Newton	Case Estates	
Weston	Mahoney's	
Winchester	Rocky Ledge Farm & Nursery	

Pleasant Valley Glads   GLADIOLI, DAHLIAS
163 Senator Ave.
Agawam, MA 01001
(Mailing address: Box 494,
Agawam, MA 01001)
(413) 786–9146; (413) 789–0307   Gary Adams, Owner

Direct retail sales; call ahead. Also mail-order sales; write for list.

When calling, get directions for sales and for display gardens.

Gary Adams and his brother Roger started their business in 1960, with excellent credentials. Both were accredited judges of the North American Gladiolus Council (NAGC)—Gary becoming one at age sixteen and Roger at seventeen—the youngest team in the NAGC. Roger—Dr. Roger Adams—head of a research department (concentrating on pests) at the University of Connecticut, eventually turned the business over to his brother.

Gary holds a Gold Medal from the NAGC for service to the gladiolus world and both brothers have received a number of awards for their flowers.

Adams does much work in growing, hybridizing, and testing glads and dahlias at Pleasant Valley and has an All-America trial garden. Some 300 new and recent gladiolus introductions are offered for sale plus dozens of dahlias. And you'll be dealing with an expert there.

The North American Gladiolus Council is very active in Massachusetts and adjoining states. If you're interested in attending shows and seminars or taking part in NAGC activities, Adams is a good person to contact.

Country House Floral   FLOWER ARRANGING MATERIALS
P.O. Box 4086, Bvl. Sta.
Andover, MA 01810
(508) 475–8463   Helga Frazzette, Owner

Direct retail sales at flower shows and symposia. Also mail-order sales; catalog $1.

Frazzette has been selling a complete line of flower arranging materials since 1974. This includes dozens of varieties of vases and containers (oriental, contemporary, classic, traditional shapes, unusual shapes, and even a half-moon hanging vase), bases and stands, pin holders, clay, foam, tape, drying materials, clippers, cutters, and many books.

If you would like to see a display of Frazzette's materials, call or write her to find out the dates and places of her scheduled flower shows and symposia.

Betsy Williams/The Proper Season   DRIED FLOWERS
68 Park St.   AND HERBS, WREATHS,
Andover, MA 01810   ARRANGEMENTS,
(Mailing address: 155 Chestnut St.,   TOPIARIES, CLASSES,
Andover, MA 01810)   BOOKS
(508) 475–2540; (508) 470–0911   Betsy Williams, Owner

Direct retail sales; open Mon.–Sat. 9:30 A.M.–5:30 P.M.; open Sun., Dec. before Christmas; closed week before Labor Day. Also mail-order sales; catalog $2.

From Boston take Rte. 93 north to exit 41, then Rte. 125 to Rte. 28 toward Andover; 4 miles from Rte. 125 is Philips Academy campus, then Rte. 28 goes down a long hill, through a blinking yellow light, and into the business center of Andover; at the first full set of lights (Chestnut St.) turn right; then take the first left onto Bartlett, and at the end of Bartlett turn right onto Park; the shop is six buildings ahead.

Betsy Williams started her business in 1969 and considering all the things she does, she's probably been busy ever since. In her shop, Betsy Williams/The Proper Season, on Park Street in downtown Andover, she sells dried herbs and flowers, books, cards, and garden accessories such as sundials, birdbaths, stone animals, and baskets.

She also sells wreaths that are works of art. Each is custom made of plant materials, most of which are grown and gathered by Williams and dried on the premises. Among her wreaths are the Faerie Ring, inspired by Botticelli's *Primavera* and made of roses, baby's breath, and thyme on a green moss-covered ring; the Fall Wreath, an interpretation of Della Robbia, in browns, creams, reds, purples, golds, and oranges; wedding wreaths with roses, single baby's breath, and statice as well as herbs and herbal flowers that have been associated with weddings since ancient times; and wreaths-for-pretty—all the wreaths that aren't named varieties. You really should see the wreaths. They are extraordinary.

Williams's workshop, teaching barn, and gardens on Chestnut Street are usually open from 9 A.M. to 3 P.M., but hours vary with the seasons, so it's best to call ahead. She holds workshops there—such as the Moss Basket Workshop, Dried Flower Nosegay Workshop, Beginning Your Herb Garden, an Evening with Basil, and an Evening with Garlic. She also gives lectures and will hold "on-the-road" workshops.

If you're in the area you might enjoy the fall open house held each year in late September or October; write or call for the exact date.

No question, this gets three stars.

Bartholomew's Cobble
Weatogue Rd.
Ashley Falls, MA 01222
(Mailing address: P.O. Box 128, Ashley Falls, MA 01222)
(413) 229–8600

Open every day, mid-Apr.–mid-Oct., 9 A.M.–5 P.M.. Naturalist on duty Wed.–Sun. Admission fee charged.

In southwestern Mass., from Sheffield follow Rte. 7 south $1\frac{1}{10}$ mile, turn right on Rte. 7A and follow directional signs to Weatogue Rd.; the entrance is on the left.

A *cobble* according to the dictionary is a naturally rounded stone, bigger than a pebble but smaller than a boulder. But Walter Pritchard Eaton, in his book *Wild Gardens of New England* (W. A. Wild Co., Boston, 1936), wrote that in the Berkshires "it is more than that with us. A cobble is a rocky hillock, or stone island, rising from the alluvial bottom lands."

Bartholomew's Cobble, rising beside the winding Housatonic River, is a natural rock garden of ferns and rare wildflowers. Approximately 800 species of plants have been cataloged there and include nearly 500 species of wildflowers; about 100 species of trees, shrubs, and vines; and some fifty-three ferns. The National Park Service of the U.S. Department of the Interior designated Bartholomew's Cobble a National Natural Landmark in 1971, and it is preserved by The Trustees of Reservations in Massachusetts (see page 230).

The cobble's nearly 6 miles of marked trails go through a very diverse habitat—from river meadows and swamps through the ferny ledges and woodlands to a summit of 1,060 feet with a view of the Housatonic valley and surrounding mountains.

The fern species and allies are thought to be the greatest natural concentration in the country. And the cobble is one of the country's most fascinating natural wild areas. A bird list, compiled since 1946, has over 236 species. It is visited by several thousand nature observers each year, including students, botanists, biologists, geologists, ecologists, foresters, photographers, and artists.

Nature walks are held in May and June and maps with self-guided tours are available at the entrance. An excellent way to get an overview of the area is the Ledges Interpretive Trail, which is an easy walk of about ½ mile in length; numbered posts along the trail correspond to numbers in a booklet that gives excellent descriptions of each area.

Build Your Own Cobble

If you're not fortunate enough to have a natural cobble, you might consider a man-made one. At Tupper Hill, the Norcross Wildlife Sanctuary—in Wales, Massachusetts, about 23 miles from Springfield, Massachusetts, and 35 miles from Hartford, Connecticut—two cobbles were made by bringing in limestone rocks and soil. These were designed for lime-loving ferns.

These cobbles and the steps in making them are described in the *Plant & Garden Handbook #59, Ferns,* available from the Brooklyn Botanic Garden (BBG), 1000 Washington Ave., Brooklyn, NY 11225-1099. The price is $3.95, plus $2.50 for postage. (Many garden centers stock the BBG handbook series.)

The book has much information on growing ferns, including an illustrated dictionary of ferns along with cultural information and climate zones.

Hartman's Herb Farm   HERBS AND PERENNIALS
Old Dana Rd.
Barre, MA 01005
(508) 355–2015   Lynn and Peter Hartman, Owners

Direct retail sales; open every day, Feb.–Dec. 24, 10 A.M.–5 P.M. Also mail-order sales; catalog $2.

Barre is northwest of Worcester; take Rte. 122 north of Barre to Old Dana Rd.; the farm is 3 miles from Rte. 122.

The Hartmans have over 250 varieties of herbs in their greenhouses and gardens along with many flowering annuals. In the shop and barn you'll find potpourri, herbs and spices, dried flower arrangements, wreaths, garden statuary, and also "The Herbal Calendar," which the Hartmans produce each year and which is sold around the country.

You're invited to browse through the display garden in its rustic, natural setting (and bring the kids to visit with Pinky Pig, the goats, sheep, rabbits, chickens, ducks, cats, and dog).

The Hartmans moved to the country in 1974 and bought a two-hundred-year-old house that hadn't been lived in for fifty years. They may be expanding their business in the future; their daughter has a degree in floriculture from the University of Massachusetts, and their son is majoring in landscape design.

The Hartmans also help customers design herb gardens and give lectures and demonstrations on herbs and dried flowers.

Sedgwick Gardens at Long Hill Reservation

572 Essex St.
Beverly, MA 01915
(508) 921–1944

Open every day, summer months, 8 A.M.–sunset. Admission fee charged.

Take Rte. 128 to exit 18; go left on Rte. 22 (Essex St.) toward Essex, 1 mile, bearing left at fork, to brick gateposts with sign.

Looking for a great place to hold a wedding? Check out the formal gardens at Long Hill Reservation. About three weddings a month are held there May to October.

Long Hill was the 114-acre summer home of Ellery and Mabel Cabot Sedgwick. When they bought the property in 1916, Mrs. Sedgwick, an experienced horticulturist and author of *The Garden Month by Month*, laid out the original gardens. She combined native pasture cedar with mountain laurel, weeping Japanese cherries, and hundreds of spring bulbs and later added lilacs, roses, and azaleas.

Further development brought a collection of tree peonies, Japanese maples, stewartias, lotuses, and other rare plants adding up to a total collection of some 400 species.

Ellery Sedgwick was editor of the *Atlantic Monthly* for twenty-nine years and guests at Long Hill included such well-known people as John Galsworthy, Bertrand Russell, and Robert Frost.

Highlights of the year are the spring plant sale, fall bulb sale, and a horticulture lecture series that is given every two weeks. The house and gardens are available to rent to garden clubs and other community groups. Tours can be arranged by appointment. For information about specific dates, courses, and rentals call or write Long Hill.

This is one of seventy-one properties of The Trustees of Reservations, dedicated to conserving the Massachusetts landscape (see page 230).

Acorn Services Corp.   REDWOOD GARDEN PRODUCTS
346 Still River Rd. (Rte. 110)
Bolton, MA 01740
(508) 779–5515   Warren K. Smith, President

Direct retail sales at factory; call ahead weekdays between 8 A.M. and 5 P.M. Also mail-order sales; color brochures and prices $2.

From Rte. I-495, west of Boston, take exit 27; go west on Rte. 117 to intersection of Rte. 110; travel north on Rte. 110 for 1 mile; the factory is on the left side.

Acorn manufactures redwood products exclusively—and has so much confidence in the durability of redwood that it offers a lifetime money-back guarantee on all of its products.

The potting benches (with stainless steel pans), display tables, plant stands, and trellises are handsome, functional, and sturdy and should please almost every gardener. These are accompanied by other gardening aids such as mud mats, plant surrounds, garden and nursery stakes, nursery flats, and lumber for adding shelves—all made from redwood.

This quality does not come without a price, but if you want top-of-the-line products—along with utility—look there.

Bow House, Inc.   GAZEBOS, OTHER GARDEN STRUCTURES
92 Randall Rd.
Bolton, MA 01740
(Mailing address: P.O. Box 228,
Bolton, MA 01740)   John J. Rogers,
(508) 779–6464   Vice President

Direct retail sales; call for appointment. Also mail-order sales; send $2 for brochures.

Take exit 27 (Bolton/Stow) on Rte. 495; go west on Main St. to Wataquadock Rd., turn left and go on Old Bay Rd. to Randall Rd.; turn right to Bow House.

"Gazebos, also called summerhouses, belvederes, and pavilions, are as old as civilization," says John Rogers of Bow House. "They are intended to be places of refreshment, light, peace, and a place to think great thoughts. A gazebo uses no energy, and it is neither sinful nor fattening."

For people who need such a place, Bow House has the solution—a gazebo kit that can be customized to the buyer's specifications. It can be open, glassed in or screened, with a deck or without, and with eight sides, six sides, or five sides. Bow House supplies a complete handbook for assembling the structure and they'll be there to answer any questions that might arise.

The company also has summerhouses, pool houses, cabanas, arched bridges, and even an insulated doghouse. The structures are unique in that they are made with curves—laminated arches, rafters, and so on—the result of Bow House's main business of making bow-roofed capes. (The garden structures part of the company began in the recession of 1982, to keep employees busy when the housing industry slowed down.)

The top-of-the-line gazebo is the Belvedeary, with a classic style and proportion, that has an elegance and grace that very few small structures have. Price, depending on options, can be well above $5,000. If price is a consideration, you might look at the Shandy; with its straight roof and simpler construction, it can go for a couple of thousand less.

For your information: *belevedere* is an Italian word for "beautiful view" and *shandy*, somewhat more plebian, is the name of a drink made with ale and lemonade.

Of Orchard Walks and Wines

How are apples, peaches, strawberries, raspberries, plums, blueberries, elderberries, and other fruits grown in Massachusetts made into serious fruit wines? Find out by touring the Nashoba Valley Orchards and Winery in Bolton, Massachusetts.

Orchardist Alenia Wagner, who has a degree in horticulture from Rutgers, conducts guided orchard walks each year, geared to home gardeners. Topics are determined by the interest and questions of participants. Wagner also gives private walks by appointment to such groups as the Massachusetts Horticultural Society and Cooperative Extension Service Master Gardeners. (The walks, of course, include tours through the winery and wine tastings.)

For a list of scheduled walks and tours call or write the Nashsoba Valley Winery, 100 Wattaquadock Hill Road, Bolton, MA 01740; (508) 779–5521. Bolton is near the junction of I-495 and Route 117, about 45 minutes west of Boston.

🦎 Isabella Stewart Gardner Museum

280 The Fenway
Boston, MA 02115
(Mailing address: 2 Palace Rd., Boston, MA 02115)
(617) 566–1401

Open Tues., 12 M.–6:30 P.M., Wed.–Sun., 12 M.–5 P.M.; closed Mon. and national holidays. Admission fee charged.

Follow Storrow Dr. to Kenmore/Fenway exit; at Kenmore Sq. turn left onto Brookline Ave., then turn left onto Longwood Ave., then left again at Palace Rd; the museum is at the corner of Palace Rd. and The Fenway. Or: *Take the E train on Green Line T to the museum stop.*

Fenway Court, built by Isabella Stewart Gardener to house the many paintings and other rarities she had collected over the years, is in the style of a fifteenth-century Venetian palace. Galleries on three floors open onto a central courtyard.

The museum is known for its collection of approximately 2,000 items, representing many cultures and spanning more than thirty centuries. It is particularly rich in its collection of Italian Renaissance paintings, including works by Botticelli, Raphael, and Titian. Also included are paintings by Rembrandt, Vermeer, Manet, Degas, Matisse, Sargent, and Whistler.

However, the horticultural highlight—making this well worth a special trip—is the central courtyard, with galleries from the three floors opening out on it. Mrs. Gardener was very fond of flowers and kept the courtyard filled with them—as it is today.

Each season brings its highlights—freesias, jasmine, and azaleas in the spring, lilies and cinerarias at Easter, chrysanthemums in the fall, and poinsettias and cyclamen at Christmas. Many varieties of orchids are on display throughout the year.

A great way to enjoy them is by having lunch or tea in the café, which overlooks the garden. A terrace is open in warm weather and you can also explore the outdoor gardens.

Greenhouse tours are held frequently and the big event of the year is the annual gardeners' greenhouse sale. Call or write for exact dates.

Newbury Perennial Gardens   PERENNIALS PLUS
65 Orchard St.
Byfield, MA 01922
(508) 462–1144   Richard A. Simkins, Owner

Direct retail sales; open every day mid-Apr.–3rd week in June, 8 A.M.–4 P.M.; Mon.–Fri., 3rd week in June–Aug., 8 A.M.–4 P.M., Sat., 8 A.M.–12 M., closed Sun. and July 4.

From I-95 take exit 55 (Central St., Byfield, Newbury exit); go east on Central St. approximately 1 mile to Orchard St.; turn left onto Orchard and go 1²/₁₀ miles to the gardens on right-hand side.

Newbury Perennial Gardens has become the destination of many perennial enthusiasts both for its huge inventory of hard-to-find plants and the opportunity to tour the personal gardens of the owner's Parker River estate. Twenty theme gardens are spread over nearly 50 acres; themes include May, geranium, grass, bog, pink, weeping, Italianate, herb, rock, and alpine.

The sales staff knows its perennials and there's a good chance that almost any request you may have for a plant—no matter how unusual—can be met.

Of special interest to perennial novices are the "planning and planting workshops" held each Saturday in May. Owner Richard Simkins narrates the history of each garden with emphasis on soil preparation. Then, with trowel in hand, everyone participates in the actual planning and planting of a border. Because these workshops are very popular, it's necessary to book well in advance.

Even if you're not interested in buying perennials or in

a workshop, the gardens, only forty minutes north of Boston, are well worth a trip.

You could wind up your visit at the popular Grog restaurant in nearby historic Newburyport, which is owned by Simkins and is decorated with bouquets from his gardens.

If You're in Cambridge . . .

Go to Harvard

Just a short distance from Harvard Square you'll find the Harvard Botanical Museum located in the University Museum building at 24 Oxford Street.

The Botanical Museum has a unique "garden of glass flowers," one of Harvard's most popular attractions. The more than 3,000 hand-blown glass flowers accurately represent more than 840 plant species and are scientifically correct to the smallest details—and they are works of art.

They were made in Germany from 1887 to 1936 by Leopold Blaschka and his son, Rudolph. You can rent a taped tour describing the history and botany of the flowers and the artistic techniques used in making them.

While you're there you may want to visit the other museums of natural history: the Mineralogical and Geological Museum, the Museum of Comparative Zoology, and the Peabody Museum of Archaeology.

The museums are open Monday through Saturday, 9 A.M. to 4:30 P.M., and Sunday, 1 P.M. to 4:30 P.M., year-round except for New Year's Day, July 4, Thanksgiving, and Christmas. Admission is charged except on Saturdays between 9 A.M. and 11 A.M.

For more information call the museums at (617) 495–3045.

Visit a Cemetery

If this isn't your idea of a pleasant thing to do it's probably because you've never been to Mount Auburn Cemetery in Cambridge, Massachusetts.

Mount Auburn, founded in 1831, was the first garden cemetery in the country. Its 170 acres have about 3,000 trees representing more than 350 varieties, almost 50,000 annuals, some 10,000 flowering bulbs, and thousands of perennials and shrubs. The hilly property also has three lakes. The area attracts many bird-watchers and hundreds of species are sighted there every year.

The grounds are open every day from 8 A.M. to 7 P.M., May through October, and from 8 A.M. to 5 P.M. the rest of the year. The address is 580 Mount Auburn Street in Cambridge, and the office phone is (617) 547–7105.

Seawright Gardens   TETRAPLOID DAYLILIES, HOSTAS
134 Indian Hill Rd. (Display Garden)
201 Bedford Rd. (Rte. 225) (Sales Garden)
Carlisle, MA 01741
(508) 369–2172   Robert D. Seawright, Owner

Direct retail sales; sales garden open every day May–June, 10:30 A.M.–4 P.M.; July–Aug., 9 A.M.–6 P.M.; open other times by appointment. The display garden is open to the public at all times. Also mail-order sales (send mail order to Indian Hill address); catalog $1.

To display garden: from Rte. 128 take Rte. 2 west to Concord; from the traffic circle in center of Concord take Lowell Rd. toward Carlisle for 3⁷/₁₀ miles to Indian Hill Rd.; turn right on to Indian Hill and go approximately ¼ mile; take the first major left at a sign that says To Autumn Ln.; follow the street around the curve to the right; the gardens are the second house on right. To sales garden: from the traffic circle in center of Carlisle take Bedford Rd. (Rte. 225) toward Bedford. Go approximately ³/₁₀ mile and turn left into 201 Bedford Rd.

"We offer some of the most spectacular varieties of modern tetraploid daylilies to be found anywhere in the world. The gardens are a sight to behold during the last half of July and early August when the daylilies are at peak bloom!"

The Massachusetts Horticultural Society (MHS) must agree; it holds an annual weekend tour of Seawright gardens each July. (Call MHS at 617–536–9280 for the exact date of the tour.)

Mr. Seawright specializes in blooms with exotic eye and blotch patterns as well as the more conventional type and has well over 300 varieties for sale. He also grows a number of varieties of hostas.

Seawright has an M.S. degree in mathematics and worked in the computer business for twenty years with such giants as Union Carbide, IBM, and Interactive Data Corp. In 1980, however, he decided that the hobby he had started as a boy of thirteen—growing daylilies—was hopelessly out of control: "Enough is enough, I said, and turned my back on the exciting world of computers."

Visit Seawright Gardens and be prepared to become a daylily addict. Chances are some of Seawright's enthusiasm will rub off on you.

Briarwood Gardens   RHODODENDRONS
14 Gully La., RFD 1,
East Sandwich, MA 02537
(508) 888–2146   Jonathan Leonard, President

Direct retail sales; open Tues.–Sun., May 1–Oct. 15, 9 A.M.–4 P.M. Also mail-order sales; catalog $1.

From Mid-Cape Hwy. (Rte. 6) take exit 3; go north 1 mile on Quaker Meetinghouse Rd. to Rte. 6A; go left on Rte. 6A for ¾ mile to Gully La.; turn left onto Gully La.; travel about ⅛ mile to Briarwood Gardens, on the right.

Briarwood Gardens, begun by Jonathan Leonard in 1983, has 150 varieties of rhododendrons for sale and has become the leading specialty house for the Dexter rhododendrons.

The gardens are only 2 miles from Heritage Plantation, the former Charles Dexter Estate, in Sandwich, Massachusetts (see pages 90–91). When Dexter retired there in 1921 he created many of the world's best hardy rhododendrons, working with English imports and tough native stock. He germinated nearly 200,000 hybrid seedlings, but he never saw many of the plants bloom because he had shipped them off to arboretums and private estates. He worked on such a scale that he created a towering collection of rhododendrons generally suited to life in the Northeast.

Leonard, working with the Heritage Plantation through the Massachusetts chapter of the American Rhododendron Society, did research on the collection and established a Dexter rhododendron nursery, Briarwood Gardens, to help give Dexter's plants the national attention they deserve. (It's a private nursery that works closely with, but is not affiliated with, Heritage Gardens.) The nursery now has over 100 named Dexter rhododendron cultivars.

Briarwood Gardens also has some Cowles hybrids, from Jack Cowles who was the horticulturist at the old Dexter Estate.

In the Sandwich area, Dexter's 'Spice,' with pink buds that open to giant white flowers, is the "King of Rhododendrons," says Leonard. This cultivar was very hard to root, and it was only through tissue culture that a good quantity of the specimen has become available. The buds are hardy to −5°F and the plant is hardy to at least −20°F.

If you have an interest in rhododendrons, Briarwood Gardens and the neighboring Heritage Plantation are a must.

Donaroma's Nursery & Landscape Services
NURSERY, LANDSCAPING

Upper Main St.
Edgartown, MA 02539
(Mailing address: Box 21898,
Edgartown, MA 02539)
(508) 627–8366

Michael Donaroma, Owner

Direct retail sales; open Mon.–Sat., year-round, 9 A.M.–5 P.M.; Sun., May–Aug., 10 A.M.–2 P.M. Also mail-order sales of wildflowers; catalog $2.

The nursery is located on Upper Main St. in Edgartown, Martha's Vineyard.

Donaroma's has a 3½-acre sales area with six greenhouses and a 9-acre farm where over 350 varieties of perennials, including wildflowers, are grown. Some of the wildflowers are not readily available elsewhere and are especially suited to the hot, sunny, dry conditions near the ocean and don't mind the wind and salt. The nursery also has orchids and other exotic flowering plants, annuals, herbs, specimen trees, and shrubs.

Michael Donaroma says his is primarily a landscape company with services ranging from the design and planning stage to a completed job—"gardens of any era or design from sod to woodland, from a Monet look to a manicured finish."

He must do good work; his client list is impressive, running the gamut from Jacqueline Onassis and Walter Cronkite to the Charlotte Inn, which is rated by some as one of the top ten inns in the United States.

But you don't have to be famous to have landscaping done by Donaroma. "If you're in need of a job," he says, "complete to the arrangement on the dining room table, call us, we'll take it on the road!"

Get a First-Hand View of Donorama's Landscaping

Spend a night, or more, at the Charlotte Inn to enjoy its landscaping and the surrounding areas of Edgarton and Martha's Vineyard as well. The inn is well known for its fine collection of antiques and for the attentive service given guests. The dining rooms are renowned for their French-American cuisine; dinners are prix fixe.

Call the inn at (508) 627–4751 for more information and to make reservations.

G. Bourne Knowles & Co., Inc.   GARDEN CENTER,
441 Washington St. (Rte. 6)   FLOWER SHOP,
Fairhaven, MA 02719   LANDSCAPING SERVICES
(Mailing address: P.O. Box 311,
Fairhaven, MA 02719)
(617) 997–8146   Bourne Knowles, President

Direct retail sales; open Mon.–Sat., year-round, 8:30 A.M.–6 P.M., Sun., 8:30 A.M.–5 P.M.; closed on major holidays; Mon.–Sat., Thanksgiving to Christmas, 8:30 A.M.–8 P.M., Sun., 8:30 A.M.–5 P.M.

About forty-five minutes from Boston and Providence, R.I., take Rte. I-195 east of New Bedford to exit 18 (Rte. 240); take Rte. 240 to Rte. 6 east; the garden center is on Rte. 6, 1⁴/₁₀ mile ahead, on the right.

You'll be able to find just about any gardening item you need— except power tools—at Knowles Garden Center and Nursery; their stock includes over 5,000 potted perennials, 180 varieties of annuals, American and European garden tools, a large variety of common and unusual trees and shrubs, and many houseplants, flowering plants, and large foliage plants. Be prepared for a lot of walking and looking. There are 10 acres of greenhouse plants.

The flower shop has fresh flower arrangements, silk and dried flowers, and even plant rentals if you don't want to commit yourself to full-time care.

In the landscape division you can contract for landscape construction, installation of sprinkling systems, tree trimming and removal, and lawn care.

Knowles holds an annual open house one weekend in

mid-May. You'll be treated to refreshments and given a chance to explore all sixteen greenhouses. Call or write for the exact date.

Cape Cod Violetry   AFRICAN VIOLETS
28 Minot St.
Falmouth, MA 02540
(508) 548–2798   John and Barbara Cook, Owners

Direct retail sales; plant shop in home; usually available 12 M.– 9 P.M., but call first. Also mail-order sales; catalog $1.

Off Rte. 28 in Falmouth Village; Minot St. is one street south of the Falmouth Hospital entrance.

The Cooks began selling African violets in 1975, and chances are very good, if you're an African violet fan, that you'll find something new here. The Cooks have over 350 varieties, many from breeders such as Lyndon Lyon, Ronn Nadeau, Winston Smith, and more, as well as some of their own hybrids.

Categories include *Saintpaulia* species, unusual striped blossoms, miniatures, semiminiatures, trailers, and standard sizes. You'll also find episcias, miniature streps, miniature sinningias, and a variety of growing supplies.

Garden in the Woods
Hemenway Rd.
Framingham, MA 01701
(508) 877–7630

Open Tues.–Sun., Apr. 15–Oct. 31, 9 A.M.–4 P.M.; closed Mon. Admission fee charged.

*Take Rte. 128 to Rte. 20 west; go 8 miles on Rte. 20 to Raymond Rd.
(second left after traffic light in South Sudbury), it's 1³/₁₀ miles to Hemenway Rd. Coming from the west on Mass. Tnpk., take exit 12 to
Rte. 9 east; go 2⁴/₁₀ miles to the Edgell Rd. exit; turn left at the light
onto Edgell Rd. (Rte. 9 overpass); travel 2¹/₁₀ miles to traffic light;
turn right onto Water St. and then take first left onto Hemenway Rd.*

This is an absolute must if you are at all interested in wildflowers. And one visit will just get you started. Spring, early summer, mid-summer, fall—you'll want to revisit the garden in every
season.

Garden of the Woods is the botanical garden of the New
England Wild Flower Society (see pages 228–229), and the largest landscaped collection of wildflowers in the Northeast.
Woodland trails meander over 45 acres, past 1,500 varieties of
plants including many rare and endangered species.

The plants flourish in a series of specially designed gardens: rich woodland groves, lily pond, sunny bog, pine barrens,
western garden, and meadow.

Beginning in early spring and continuing through late
fall garden displays are an ever-changing kaleidoscope of wildflowers, shrubs, and trees. In April you'll see hepaticas and
trailing arbutus; in May, yellow lady's slippers and trilliums; June
brings out prickly pear cactus and pitcher plants; turk's cap lilies and blazing stars take the stage in July; followed by cardinal
flowers and turtleheads in August; and then asters and gentians
and brilliant foliage in September and October.

At the visitor's center you can get information about self-
guided trails or arrange to take an informal walk with a guide
on Tuesday or Friday mornings at 10 A.M. The library here has
New England Wild Flower Society publications as well as slide
programs for rent. There's also a book and gift shop and a plant
sales area.

One of the highlights of the year is the annual plant sale,
held the second Saturday in June.

Weston Nurseries

E. Main St. (Rte. 135)
(Mailing address: P.O. Box 186,
Hopkinton, MA 01748)
(508) 435–3414; within Mass.:
1 (800) 322–2002   R. Wayne Mezitt, President

Direct retail sales; open Mon.–Sat., Apr. 1–Oct. 28, 8 A.M.–6 P.M.; Oct. 30–Dec. 23, 8 A.M.–5 P.M.; Dec. 27–Mar. 31, 8 A.M.–4:30 P.M.; open on Sun. only from Apr. 16–June 18; closed most national holidays.

Take Rte. 495 to exit 21A (W. Main St.) to Rte. 135 to Hopkinton Center; Weston Nurseries is about 1 mile past the traffic light on the left.

Founded in 1923 by Peter J. Mezitt, Weston Nurseries calls for superlatives. Its "Visitor's Guide" (pick up a copy at the garden center) says that it grows the largest variety of landscape-size plants, shrubs, and trees in New England—and perhaps in the entire United States.

Some statistics: almost 1,000 acres, fourteen greenhouses for propagation, over 500,000 container-grown plants, and over 5 million plants in the fields. The varieties grown include more than 2,000 evergreens, 250 deciduous trees, 500 shrubs, and 1,000 perennials.

Over 95 percent of plants sold are propagated and grown in fields in Hopkinton. The average plant is over seven years old before its size and quality are considered good enough to be sold. So during its growth, it's been exposed repeatedly to the temperature and climate extremes of Hopkinton weather.

Weston Nurseries puts out a large catalog each year with excellent plant descriptions and cultural information. You can get a copy at the nursery or call to have one sent to you (no charge).

The large garden center at Weston is staffed by professional horticulturists who are able to answer or research most questions. In addition to plant material, the center stocks gardening needs including lawn and garden products and garden accessories and gifts.

The staff of Weston Nurseries takes an active interest in integrated pest management (IPM), which is based on restrained use of pesticides and substitution of environmentally safe alternatives—such as beneficial insects. Over the past ten years, as Weston has made an effort to cut back on poisons, bird life has increased substantially on Weston's acreage. Some quite rare birds are making a comeback, and in the garden center there's an up-to-date list of species sighted for the many bird-watchers who visit regularly.

Corliss Bros. Inc.   GARDEN CENTER, NURSERY
31 Essex Rd., Rte. 133
Ipswich, MA 01938
(508) 356–5422   Steven Walfield, General Manager

Direct retail sales; open Mon.–Sat., Jan.–Mar., 8 A.M.–5 P.M.; Mon.–Sat., Apr.–June, 7 A.M.–6 P.M., Sun. 10 A.M.–4 P.M.; Mon.–Sat., July–Sept., 7 A.M.–5 P.M.; Mon.–Sat., Oct.–Dec., 7 A.M.–5 P.M., Sun. 10 A.M.–4 P.M.

Take Rte. 128, north of Boston, to Rte. 1-A north, then to Rte. 133 east.

Corliss Bros. is an exceptionally complete garden center where you can find shrubs, trees, perennials, annuals, vegetables, statuary, fertilizers, pesticides, herbicides, tools, books, houseplants, mulch, sod, railway ties, planting soils, pottery, bonsai, bird food, bird feeders, and grass seed.

Did we miss anything? Oh yes, they also offer landscaping services, have a large variety of dwarf and unusual plant material, and are the originators of 'Emerald' euonymus.

One final thing: they emphasize quality, variety, and service. A good place to go.

John Messelaar Bulb Co., Inc.   HOLLAND IMPORTED
150 County Rd., Rte. 1-A.   BULBS
Ipswich, MA 01930
(Mailing address: P.O. Box 269,
Ipswich, MA 01930)
(508) 356–3737   C. Pieter Messelaar, President

Direct retail sales at warehouse; open Mon.–Sat., Sept.–Dec. 15, 9 A.M.–6 P.M., Sun., 1 P.M.–6 P.M. Also mail-order sales; free catalog.

Take Rte. 128 north to Rte. 1-A north; the company is on Rte. 1-A in Ipswich.

Since its founding in 1946 by John Messelaar, the company has been importing top-quality bulbs from various farmers in Holland and selling them in the United States in both retail and wholesale quantities. Bulbs include hyacinths, tulips, daffodils, narcissi, crocus, iris, scilla, allum, anemones, snowdrops, freesias, daylilies, and more.

The warehouse in Ipswich is open from September through December 15 and carries a complete stock of all bulbs. By buying in larger quantities you can get a good price break.

The Arnold Arboretum of Harvard University
125 Arborway
Jamaica Plain, MA 02130–2795
(617) 524–1718; (617) 524–1717 (for recorded information about current exhibits, special events)

Grounds open daily sunrise to sunset; Hunnewell Visitor Center inside main gate on Arborway open Mon.–Fri., 9 A.M.–4 P.M. (except holidays), Sat.–Sun., 10 A.M.–4 P.M.; Dana Greenhouses open to the public Wed., 1:30 P.M.–4 P.M.

Take Huntington Ave. (toward Brookline) to Rte. 1 south; follow Rte. 1 south to Rte. 203 (Arborway).

Established in 1872, the Arnold Arboretum is the oldest arboretum in the country designed for both university and public use. Although first owned by Harvard, in 1888 the university bequeathed it to the Boston Park System, which then leased the land back to Harvard for $1 a year, bound by a 999-year lease.

Frederick Law Olmsted was largely responsible for designing the arboretum with winding paths and roads that allow close access to the collections.

The 265-acre arboretum has more than 7,000 kinds of trees and shrubs from around the world, and because it is a center for scientific study, it has introduced more than 2,000 new plants. Among them are the paperbark maple, the dove tree, the Korean mountain ash, the Arnold dwarf forsythia, and the Japanese tree lilac.

Plaques with scientific and common names are on or near many of the plants, and if you want further information about them the Hunnewell Visitor Center contains thousands of books, journals, pamphlets, and photos that will help you.

For a first visit it's a good idea to pick up a map and try one of the self-guided tours, such as the Chinese Path with its hundreds of species from China that now grow in the arboretum or the two-mile Sargent Trail, which leads visitors through the arboretum's more naturalistic areas and diverse plant habitats. The arboretum is in hardiness Zone 6 of the U.S. Department of Agriculture and in Zone 5 of the Arnold Arboretum hardiness map.

One of the highlights of the year is "Lilac Sunday" when more than 400 varieties of fragrant lilacs are in bloom and people are invited to come, enjoy the blooms, and have a picnic. (Sorry, no picnics at other times.)

But there are many other events around the year; to get a list of them send a self-addressed stamped envelope (SASE) to the Public Affairs Department of the aboretum. An educational program with classes, workshops, tours, and exhibits is held year-round; call for a brochure. Guided tours are scheduled on Sundays at 2 P.M. in the spring and fall and special tours may be scheduled with two weeks' advance reservations.

Visit the Victory Garden East

Get a firsthand view of the Victory Garden East, made famous on PBS television by the late James Crockett and now presented by Bob Thomson. The garden is at Lexington Gardens, 93 Hancock St., Lexington, MA 02173. (The phone is 617-862–7000.) It's open Monday through Saturday, April through November, and you're welcome any time except when the garden is being photographed.

Lexington Gardens, where the Victory Garden is located, is a large garden center/nursery where, one spokesman says, you can find everything "from A to Z." "If we don't have it," he says, "it isn't."

Hours at Lexington Gardens are 9 A.M. to 5 P.M., Monday through Saturday except during the spring—when it's open Monday through Friday, 8 A.M. to 8 P.M., and on Saturdays from 8 A.M. to 6 P.M. The gardens are easy to find—just ¼ mile from the historic Lexington battle site.

Note: for an update on *Crockett's Victory Garden* get a copy of Bob Thomson's *The New Victory Garden.* Ten years of new vegetable gardening techniques are presented with more than 200 color photographs and 336 pages of text.

Wilson Farm, Inc.
10 Pleasant St.
Lexington, MA 02173
(617) 862–3900

FARM AND GARDEN TOURS,
GARDEN CENTER

Operated by Wilson family since 1884

Direct retail sales; open Mon., Wed., Thurs., Sat., year-round, 9 A.M.–6 P.M., Fri., 9 A.M.–8 P.M., Sun., 9 A.M.–5:30 P.M.; closed Tues.

From Rte. 128, near Boston, take exit 29-A to Rte. 2 east; from Rte. 2, take the Pleasant St. exit, going left under Rte. 2; the farm is 1 mile ahead on Pleasant St.

Wilson Farm is primarily a market and garden center, selling produce grown on the farm's 250 acres along with cut flowers; flowering and foliage plants; flats of annuals, perennials, and vegetables; gardening supplies; dried flowers; bird food and feeders; and more. Also on the premises are some 5,000 laying hens that supply customers with farm-fresh eggs.

Wilson Farm includes a dairy farm in Maine, another retail market on 150 acres in Litchfield, New Hampshire, and a total of sixteen greenhouses and over 100 full-time employees. Among the employees are eleven Wilson family members.

Of particular interest to gardeners are the popular guided tours that give a behind-the-scenes view of the operations. The tour covers growing fields, greenhouses, food preparation, and storage areas and an in-depth view of the vegetable fields. The Massachusetts Horticultural Society sponsors an annual tour and other groups are welcome. Call the farm for information about scheduling a group visit.

Ludlow Herb Farm
943 Center St. (Rte. 21)
Ludlow, MA 10156
(413) 589–9875

HERBS, HERBAL PRODUCTS,
PERENNIALS, CLASSES

Charles Stickney, Owner

Direct retail sales; open Thurs.–Sun., mid-Apr.–Christmas, 9 A.M.–5:30 P.M.; other hours by chance—call ahead. Also mail-order sales (no plants); write for catalog.

Take Ludlow exit (exit 7) on Mass. Tnpk., go north 2⅓ mile on Rte. 21. (Parking is in the backyard; enter from Lyons St.)

After retiring from his retail florist business Stickney started Ludlow Herb Farm as a "part-time activity." To his surprise he found the herb business kept him as busy as ever.

You'll find a large number of herb plants, assorted heaths and heathers, pot grown *red* daylilies, some of the rarer forms of fox gloves, and a great many perennial geraniums. Stickney also has bulk dried herbs and spices, essential and fragrance oils, potpourri, a number of herbal gift items, dried flowers, and some 50 books on herbs.

One of the most popular features of Ludlow Herb Farm is the classes, which are held throughout the year. These include basket making, wreaths, straw hats, potpourri, and—the most popular—soap making. In this class, a homecrafter will show you how to make soap with an emphasis on scents and fragrances. Stickney also gives hour-long lectures for groups.

The old building that houses the shops was built and operated as a tavern until 1848. It has nine fireplaces and a beehive oven. Every year Stickney holds an open house, with the entire building open, from Thanksgiving Day through the following Sunday. Guest artisans and craftsmen give numerous demonstrations throughout the weekend.

An exhibition garden of herbs with identification labels is in the yard of the farm. Every Saturday morning, in season, Stickney holds a garden walk for plant identification. The garden is at its best after May 30, but visit earlier to enjoy spring bulbs and wildflowers. Around July 4, approximately 100 varieties of daylilies (appropriately red) are in bloom.

And finally, the farm has a noncirculating garden reference library, which can be used during regular hours or by appointment.

Olde Gardens Co. DECORATIVE GARDEN ANTIQUES
1305 Blue Hill Ave.
Mattapan, MA 02126
(617) 296–0445 Jorge Epstein, Owner

Direct retail (and wholesale) sales from warehouse. Open by appointment; get directions when calling.

Jorge Epstein has an intense interest in gardening and with antiques associated with gardening. Since 1938, he says, he has been making an effort "to offer very exceptional material of interest to people who understand what makes a great garden."

This includes columns, urns, gates, sculpture, furniture, lighting, architectural fragments, pedestals, gazebos, fountains, benches, slate, granite, terra-cotta tile, and wrought iron.

If any of the above interest you, a trip to Epstein's warehouse should be rewarding.

Visit a "Teaching" Farm

Green Tree Farm, on Brush Hill Road in Merrimac, Massachusetts, is really a "teaching" farm according to Walter and Nancy Perkins, proprietors.

"We offer garden tours," they say, "lectures and demonstrations with herbs and dry flowers, and highlight three seasonal events. It's a beautiful 12-acre unspoiled farm in the country with woods, gardens, a pond, and loads of fresh air."

Green Tree Farm is open Fridays and Saturdays, 10 A.M. to 5 P.M., always by appointment. The annual May festival, on a Saturday in mid-May, is one of the special events of the year. The Perkinses have many herb plants for sale at that time along with a number of perennials. Usually they have about three dozen craftspeople par-

ticipating—potters, weavers, folk artists, antiquers, calligraphers—
even morris dancers.

If you're interested, the Perkinses have brochures about the
Green Tree Farm and a newsletter, which they will send on request.
Their address and phone number are Brush Hill Rd., Merrimac, MA
01860; (508) 346–9540.

Wyrttun Ward
HERB AND WILDFLOWER PLANTS

18 Beach St.
Middleboro, MA 02346
(508) 866–4087

Gilbert and Annette Bliss, Owners

Direct retail sales; open every day, May–June, 10 A.M.–6 P.M.;
other times call ahead. Also mail-order sales; catalog $1.

*Take Rte. 495 (near New Bedford) to exit 2; turn north toward Carver,
then take an immediate left on Rte. 58 (Beach St.); Wyrttun Ward is
1¼ miles ahead.*

Wryttun is an Anglo-Saxon word meaning "herbs" and the verb
ward means "to tend or keep." "In this sense," says Gilbert Bliss,
"we keep alive the culture and knowledge of herbalists, which
has existed over the centuries."

A few years ago, when the Bliss family was forced, for
health reasons, to find alternatives to refined sugars, salts, and
food additives, they began growing culinary herbs. This led to
more herbs and wildflowers as well, and currently Wyrttun Ward
has over eighty varieties of herb plants and over fifty wildflower
plants.

The Blisses suggest a number of garden collections, including the dyer's garden, the culinary garden, Shakespeare's
garden, a sorceror's garden (this includes skullcap, rue, may-
apple, and aconite), and the zodiac garden.

🌱 The Botanic Garden of Smith College

College La.
Northampton, MA 01063
(413) 585–2748

Greenhouse open every day, 8 A.M.–4:15 P.M.; arboretum open at all times.

Take Northampton exit on Rte. 91; Smith College is located on Mass. Rte. 9 just northwest of the city center.

The entire 160-acre campus of Smith College is an arboretum, with botany listed as one of the four sciences to which "particular attention will be paid" in the first college circular issued in September 1872.

In the early 1890s a landscape firm was asked to design a comprehensive plan for the campus, and in 1895 the plan was completed by Frederick Law Olmsted.

Probably the best way to see the arboretum is first to stop at the Lyman Plant House (or greenhouse) on College Lane to pick up a map and guidebook. While you're there you might tour the greenhouse, the first portion of which was built in 1895 and which was expanded through the early 1980s. It consists of a warm temperate house, a cool temperate house, a palm house, an acacia and succulent house, and propagating houses, as well as rooms for botany classes.

Allow plenty of time and plan to do lots of walking to see the campus arboretum. With the map and guidebook, you'll be able to enjoy the more than 1,000 varieties of trees and shrubs as well as the many gardens setting off the architecture of the college buildings. This was part of the original purpose of the campus—to provide not only education and research, but also pleasure.

Annual events at the Lyman Plant House are the chrysanthemum show, beginning the first Saturday in November, and the bulb show, which opens the first Saturday in March.

Gladside Gardens   GLADIOLI, DAHLIAS
61 Main St.
Northfield, MA 01360
(413) 498—2657   Corys M. Heselton, Owner

Direct retail sales; open every day, summer and fall, 9 A.M.—7
P.M.; in winter, by appointment. Also mail-order sales; send $1 for list.

*Take Rte. 63 north from Rte. 202, or Rte. 10 north from Rte. 91, to
Northfield; the gardens are on Main St., on right side when traveling
north.*

Heselton has been growing and selling glads, dahlias, mums,
perennials, houseplants, succulents, and more for over fifty years.
If you have any questions or problems with these plants he'll be
glad to help you—and with that extensive background, his advice should be good. He is well known in horticultural circles
and has been highly recommended by many plant societies. He
sells plants to a number of foreign countries as well as to all
fifty states and Canada.

Currently Heselton is working on propagating and hybridizing some fragrant South African glads with other fragrant
glads and hopes to produce some with notable scents.

Heselton and his wife are planning to sell the business
and take things a little easier. But not to worry—Gladside Gardens will probably still be there; Heselton plans to help and
advise the new owners on continuing the business.

Sunburst Show Gardens   GLADIOLI, DAHLIAS
357 Winthrop St. (Rte. 44)
P.O. Box 457
Rehoboth, MA 02769
(508) 252—3259   Edna and Wilfrid Dufresne, Owners

Direct retail sales; open from the first spring flowers to first frost in fall, usually 8 A.M.–6 P.M.; it's best to call first. Also mail-order sales; send large self-addressed stamped envelope (SASE) for catalog.

The gardens are located on Rte. 44, 1¹/₁₀ miles west of the traffic light at the intersection of Rte. 118 and Rte. 44. Coming from Providence, R.I., they are just before the 5-mile marker on Rte. 44.

The aim of the Dufresnes is to make Sunburst Show Gardens— by good planning and gardening practices and by growing the finest varieties—a flower garden for connoisseurs. Using the best glads of hybridizers from around the country, over 300 gladiolus seedlings are tested each season and 400 varieties of champion stock are grown.

Along with glads, the Dufresnes are testing 100 seedlings of dahlias and have over forty varieties of tricolor dahlias under cultivation each season. One of their seedlings, 'Sunburst Nelson,' with bright yellow and orange flowers, won numerous awards including ten tricolors and five achievement awards from the American Dahlia Society before its recent introduction.

The Dufresnes know their flowers; both are accredited judges of the North American Gladiolus Council and the American Dahlia Society. Contact them if your group might be interested in slide presentations of glads and dahlias.

Sunburst Show Gardens are open for visitors during the bloom season (please phone ahead). And you can go away with some cut flowers—they're usually available during the growing season.

Tranquil Lake Nursery, Inc.   DAYLILIES, IRIS, SEDUM
45 River St.
Rehoboth, MA 02769   Philip A. Boucher and
(508) 252–4310; (508) 336–6491   Warren P. Leach, Partners

Direct retail sales; open Mon.–Sat., May 1–late Nov., 9 A.M.–5 P.M. Also mail-order sales; catalog 25 cents.

*Take Rte. 195 east of Providence, R.I., to exit 1 in Mass.—not R.I.;
from the exit, take Rte. 114A north to the intersection with Rte. 44; go
east on Rte. 44 to River St., turn left onto River St.; the nursery is the
fourth house on the right; watch for the sign.*

Tranquil Lake offers daylilies (diploids, tetraploids, doubles, and
minis), Japanese and Siberian iris, sedum, and many other perennials and ornamental plants.

The daylily collection includes the old and well-known
and some of the very new. The nursery serves as an outlet for
daylily breeders in New England and other parts of the country
and is also developing its own breeding program. While only
about 500 plants are listed in the catalog, the nursery usually
has a few thousand others available with new ones added each
year.

People are welcome to walk through the nursery and the
several display areas. Bloom seasons are as follows: Siberian iris,
mid-May through June, peak about June 1; Japanese iris, mid-
June through July, peak about July 7; and daylilies, mid-May
to October, peak about July 20.

Both partners have a strong background of plant and
nursery experience (a combined total of over forty years). Warren Leach is recognized as a top-notch landscape designer and
has given programs and seminars at the Arnold Arboretum and
Radcliffe College, among others. He also gives garden lectures
and slide presentations.

Philip Boucher adds, "Perhaps you could mention that
inquiries about plants and gardening are welcomed and we will
try our best to answer what gardening questions come our way."

Nor'East Miniature Roses, Inc.   MINIATURE ROSES
58 Hammond St.
Rowley, MA 01969
(508) 948–7964; outside Mass.
1 (800) 426–6485

F. Harmon Saville, Owner

Direct retail sales; open every day, year-round, 8 A.M.–4:30 P.M. Also mail-order sales; free catalog.

Take Rte. 95 (north from Boston, south from N.H.) to Rte. 133; go east on Rte. 133 to Rte. 1A north; go north about ½ mile; take a right at the first set of lights (drugstore on corner) onto Hammond St.

Nor'East Miniature Roses, started in 1972 by F. Harmon Saville, was, according to an insider, "the result of a hobby gone wild"! A year after he started growing miniatures in his basement he had over 150 plants and it got to the point where his friends were making excuses when he tried to give them away. So selling the plants was the next logical step. Today he sells almost a million a year.

In the rose world, an All-America award is the Nobel Prize of rose growing. A few are awarded each year by All-America Rose Selections (AARS), an organization of wholesale rose growers who have twenty trial gardens around the country, representing almost every climate. Roses are scored by trial judges over a period of two years and there usually are several winners each year. In 1989 the AARS chose Saville's miniature 'New Beginning' plus another miniature rose, from Conard-Pyle, as the first two miniatures ever to win this prestigious award.

Miniature roses have grown in popularity in recent years, one reason being, as a class, they're hardier than hybrid teas and also more disease resistant.

"Here in Rowley where the winters can get really rough," says Saville, "we merely rake a foot-deep layer of oak leaves onto the beds and have no winter kill."

The little roses bloom profusely from early summer to Thanksgiving and grow to an average of 12–18 inches, with some only 5–8 inches tall. This makes them ideal for growing in small spaces, even in a city apartment.

Nor'East has about 100 varieties of minis listed in the catalog but many more are available in Rowley. And while you're in Rowley you can visit Nor'East's All-America Rose Selections display garden as well as the company's miniature rose display and test gardens.

F. W. Schumacher Co., Inc.   TREE AND SHRUB SEEDS
36 Spring Hill Rd.
Sandwich, MA 02563–1023   David W. Allen and
(617) 888–0659   Donald H. Allen, Owners

   Mail-order sales only; catalog $1.

F. W. Schumacher Co. has been selling tree and shrub seeds for over sixty years and has, to put it conservatively, a *very* extensive inventory.

   For example, under *Betula* (birch), you'll find these listings: *B. albo, B. fontinalis, B. ermani, B. jaquemontiana, B. lenta, B. lutea, B. maximowicziana, B. nigra, B. papyrifera, B. pendula, B. platphylla japonica, B. populifolia,* and *B. utillis.* You get the idea. And the list of birches is not nearly as lengthy as many others.

   If you're inclined to pass this up as being too specialized, think twice. If you have patience—which you'll need—you may find it fascinating. The catalog is filled with suggestions, and when you send for a copy, it would be a good idea to include an extra dollar for the booklet, *How to Grow Seedlings of Trees and Shrubs.*

   Good luck!

Heritage Plantation of Sandwich
Pine and Grove Sts., Box 566
Sandwich, MA 02563
(508) 888–3300

   Open every day, mid-May–Oct., 10 A.M.–5 P.M. Admission fee charged.

The plantation is 3 miles from the Cape Cod Sagamore Bridge; exit on Rte. 6A; then take Rte. 130 to Pine St. to the plantation.

The gardens at Heritage Plantation have been called one of the finest rhododendron displays in the world. The plantation is on a 76-acre site, the former estate of Charles O. Dexter, a New Bedford mill owner, who became famous as a rhododendron breeder.

When Dexter retired at the age of fifty-nine he started plant breeding and in the remaining twenty-two years of his life he developed between 5,000 and 10,000 new rhododendron seedlings each year. As parent stock, he used tough native rhododendrons along with English hybrids and exotic foreign species. Although he was an expert plant breeder, he was a poor record keeper, and most of his plants were distributed without records or names.

Over the years, American Rhododendron Society members have worked to locate and name the best and propagate them for distribution. As a result there are now 145 known Dexter cultivars.

The thousands of rhododendrons at Heritage Plantation, along with other flowering evergreens, bloom in May, June, and July. In the summer, over 700 varieties of daylilies take over. Throughout the landscaped grounds, flower beds, and nature trails there are more than 1,000 varieties of trees, shrubs, and flowers, all labeled. This provides a horticultural education in itself.

Someone once said about the plantation, "The view is almost unbelievable! Dazzling arrays of azaleas and rhododendrons stretching as far as the eye can see."

The remainder of Heritage Plantation may be overshadowed by the horticultural displays. But there are many exhibits of Americana—vintage cars, Indian artifacts, firearms, military miniatures, a museum store, a working windmill that grinds grain, a display of early tools, an old-fashioned carousel that

has been restored and runs, a large collection of Currier and
Ives lithographs, and a multitude of folk arts.

The plantation has a number of courses, lectures, workshops, and tours throughout the year, many on horticulture.
Call or write to be placed on the mailing list.

Michelin's *Guide to New England* gives Heritage Plantation three stars. What more can we say.

Tripple Brook Farm   WIDE VARIETY OF PLANTS—
37 Middle Rd.   PRODUCTIVE, EDIBLE, UNDERUTILIZED
Southampton, MA 01073
(413) 527–4626   Stephen Breyer, Owner

Direct retail sales; "We are usually here—call before coming."
Also mail-order sales; free catalog (or list if catalogs are all gone).

*Southampton is about 8 miles northwest of Springfield; get exact direc-
tions when calling.*

Breyer says that, primarily, he sells "small potted plants." He
became interested in gardening and collecting plants partly out
of a desire to make the best use of his farm property—to grow
and use the most productive, interesting, and attractive plants.
In the process, he says, he found that many worthwhile plants
are being underutilized and aren't available from commercial
nurseries. Use of the plants on his farm became the basis for
the plants he sells.

"A complete list of worthy plants that can be grown in
temperate climates would include many thousands of species. I
feel that I have scarcely scratched the surface of the vast range
of plant material."

He has arranged his plants by uses, and it's quite a list.
Here are some examples. *Edible fruits* include fig, ground cherry,
Indian strawberry, mulberry, and prickly pear. Some *other edi-
bles* are bamboo shoots, mint watercress, and wild ginger. Among

the *wildlife foods* are low bush blueberry, hardy kiwi, and Virginia creeper. *Ground covers* include bluets, coltsfoot, moneywort, and speedwell. *For poor, dry locations* try artemisia, sedum, or hen and chickens. Some plants *for wet locations* are aster, cattail, marsh fern, and sweet flag and *for shady locations,* bamboo, ferns, fringed loosestrife, sheep laurel, sweet woodruff, and wintergreen.

He has other categories such as fragrant flowers, trees and shrubs, vines, hedges, screens, and barriers.

A good way to become acquainted with all this plant material is to get a catalog—which is packed with information—and study it before going to the farm. At the farm you will find many more plants that haven't yet been cataloged.

Among the most popular plants currently, says Breyer, are the various species of hardy bamboos, hardy kiwi fruit, and a few other fruits, mostly less well-known types.

Interesting.

New England Bonsai Gardens, Inc.   BONSAI
89 Pleasant St.
South Natick, MA 01760   Wayne Schoech and
(508) 653–6330   Hitoshi Kanegae, Owners

Direct retail sales; open Mon.–Sat., 9 A.M.–6 P.M., Sun., 10 A.M.–5 P.M. Mail-order sales are planned for the future.

Take Rte. 90 to Rte. 126; go south to South Natick; the gardens are on Pleasant St. south of Rte. 16 in South Natick.

New England Bonsai Gardens is a wholesale bonsai business, but has a retail sales section in its greenhouse. You'll find bonsai tools, pots, soil, fertilizer, trees, and starter plants.

The company often has sales, when you can get especially good buys; watch for ads in area newspapers or call to get sales schedule.

hire Garden Center

nte. 102
Stockbridge, MA 01262
(Mailing address: Box 826, Stockbridge, MA 01262)
(413) 298–3926

Open every day, year-round, 10 A.M.–5 P.M. Admission charged
May 1–Oct. 15.

*The garden center is located 2 miles west of the center of Stockbridge,
at the intersection of Rtes. 102 and 183.*

Begun in 1934, the Berkshire Garden Center is a nonprofit 15-
acre botanic garden, designed to both educate and provide
enjoyment. Shrubs, trees, flowers, herbs, and vegetables are
labeled for easy identification, and a map of the gardens, available at the visitors' center, will help you find your way around.

Plantings include primroses, conifers, daylilies, perennials, shrubs, everlasting flowers, herbs, and vegetables. There
are a number of small, landscaped gardens, a rose garden, a
terraced herb garden, ponds, a woodland walk, and a wildflower walk.

A passive-solar greenhouse and a sunpit greenhouse show
how cool-season vegetables can be grown throughout the winter without use of fuel.

The visitors' center houses a resource library, which has
reference materials and a large collection of seed catalogs. You
can also browse through an herb products shop and a garden
gift shop. A horticultural staff is always available for answering
questions.

The center has a number of events throughout the year,
including a daffodil show (last weekend in April), a plant fair,
offering many types of plants for sale (mid-May), an herb fair
(mid-June), a flower show (mid-August), and a harvest festival

(first Saturday in October). Call or write for specific dates and times.

🌿 Naumkeag

Prospect Hill Rd.
Stockbridge, MA 01262
(Mailing address: P.O. Box 792, Stockbridge, MA 01262)
(413) 298–3239

Open every day, Memorial Day to Columbus Day, 10 A.M.–4:30 P.M. Admission fee charged.

Take I-90 to Rte. 102; at the intersection of Rte. 102 and Rte. 7, at the Red Lion Inn, take Pine St. north; bear left on Prospect Hill Rd., go ½ mile to entrance, on left.

Naumkeag, the summer home of Joseph H. Choate (1832–1917), has a twenty-six-room mansion, designed by Stanford White, furnished with rare antiques, china, and paintings, which is open to the public. But for many visitors, the highlight of the estate is the extensive gardens. Landscape architect Fletcher Steele designed them and they gradually were completed over a period of thirty years.

The gardens include the Afternoon Garden, which was planned as an outdoor room; the Linden walk, an archway of some sixty trees; a topiary garden; a brick-walled Chinese Garden; and a tile-roofed temple, which presides over the landscape.

On the second Thursday of the month, from June through September, special garden tours are held, starting at 6 P.M. Reservations are required as the tours are very popular.

Naumkeag is one of the properties of The Trustees of Reservations (see page 230) and is also on the National Register of Historic Places.

🦎 Old Sturbridge Village

1 Old Sturbridge Rd.
Sturbridge, MA 01566
(508) 347–3362

Open Tues.–Sun., Jan. 1–Apr. 30, 10 A.M.–4 P.M.; every day, May 1–Oct. 31, 9 A.M.–5 P.M.; every day, Nov. 1–Nov. 30, 10 A.M.–4 P.M.; Tues.–Sun., Dec. 1–Dec. 31, 10 A.M.–4 P.M.; closed Christmas and New Year's Day. Admission fee charged.

On Rte. 20 west; from Mass. Tnpk. (I-90) take exit 9; from I-84 take exit 2.

When you enter Old Sturbridge Village it's easy to imagine you're back in a New England village of the 1830s. On its more than 200 acres are some forty buildings that have been moved to the village from all over New England and carefully restored.

Of special interest to gardeners are the kitchen gardens, growing early nineteenth-century vegetables, fruit trees, and field crops typical of this period; an herb garden; a working farm; and formal flower gardens.

During garden days, in early August, you can see the gardens in full bloom—flowers, vegetables, and herbs. At this time there also are slide talks about gardening, workshops, demonstrations on food preservation techniques, guided tours, and more. In other seasons, special events range from maple sugaring to cider making.

To get year-round information about events, write to Old Sturbridge Village, Marketing and Communication Department, Sturbridge, MA 01566-0200, and ask to be put on the calendar mailing list.

A & P Orchids   ORCHIDS

110 Peters Rd.
Swansea, MA 02777
(508) 675–1717   **Azhar and Penny Mustafa, Owners**

Direct retail sales; open Mon.–Sat., year-round, 10 A.M.–4:30 P.M. Also mail-order sales; free listing (note: a color catalog is planned and a charge will be made).

Take I-95 to Providence, R.I., then take I-195 east to Mass.; take exit 3 to Rte. 6, go west for 1¼ miles and bear right off Rte. 6 at Kents; then take first right, then second left onto Peters Rd.; it's at the end of the road, on the left.

After growing orchids in their home, the Mustafas started their business in 1985. They offer their own hybrids, with an emphasis on very long-lasting flowers—two to three months. Among them are *Paphiopedilum* species, primary and complex hybrids; also species of *Phalaenopsis, Cattleya,* and more. A & P Orchids is now the home of the Mt. Madonna Collection.

The Mustafas do all their own laboratory work and have small seedlings available in flasks. Although they now have a greenhouse, because of their experience in growing orchids in their home they can offer firsthand advice to others who are interested in home growing.

The Walt Nicke Co.   GARDEN ITEMS
36 McLeod La.
Topsfield, MA 01983
(Mailing address: P.O. Box 433,
Topsfield, MA 01983)
(508) 887–3388   Katrina Nicke Neefus, Owner

Mail-order sales; write for catalog. (Hopes to open a retail shop in the future.)

If you read garden magazines you've probably seen the Walt Nicke ads, which have been appearing for more than twenty-five years. The company has over 300 gardening items, many imported. Among them are Sheffield hand-forged garden tools;

grub and gooseneck hoes; Audubon bird calls; Scottish plant support rings; the famous Cape Cod Weeder that's served generations of gardeners; the Small Wonder pocket pruner; propagators and pots; sprinklers; thatched roof birdhouses; and sheepskin garden gloves.

There are also English Solo Sprayers, which operate something like a trombone and which started the late Walt Nicke in his business. Nicke was a rose grower and back in the 1960s when he couldn't find a sprayer that didn't clog or break down he put together a do-it-yourself spray rig. Then he came across the English Solo Sprayer, which he liked so well that he decided to import it for American gardeners. Soon he put out a catalog of gardening aids—every one of which he had personally used and found handy.

The company is now operated by his daughter, Katrina Nicke Neefus, and is doing better than ever. The catalog has added products and each issue (two per year) contains an article on a specific gardening topic.

Neefus, you might say, has kept gardening in the family. Her husband, Dr. Chris Neefus, is a botanist with the University of New Hampshire.

Very interesting catalog. Worth writing for.

Rock Spray Nursery, Inc.
Holsbery Rd.
Truro, MA 02666
(Mailing address: P.O. Box 693,
Truro, MA 02666)
(508) 349–6769

HEATHS, HEATHERS,
SEASHORE PLANTINGS

Betsy Erickson and
Kate Herrick, Owners

Direct retail sales; open every day in season, usually 9 A.M.–5 P.M., but hours vary seasonally; please call ahead for appointment. Also mail-order sales; free catalog.

On Cape Cod between Wellfleet and Provincetown; take Pamet Rd. exit off Rte. 6 in Truro, go under the bridge and take a left at the stop sign; take a right on Depot Rd.; the nursery is there, next to Down Cape Realty.

"Because our interest lies in the *growing* of plants and not just redistribution," says Kate Herrick, "we concentrate on the types of plant that interest us. We are acquiring new species of *Calluna* (heather) and *Erica* (heath) to test in our gardens for both hardiness and appeal. Most of the plants we grow are propagated from cuttings and grown in pots."

This is definitely a place to go if you are interested in heaths and heathers. Among the many varieties at Rock Spray are *Calluna vulgaris* (Ling or Scotch heather), *Daboecia* varieties (Irish heather), *Erica carnea* (winter heath), *Erica cinerea* (bell heather or twisted heath), *Erica vagans* (Cronish heath), *Bruckenthalia spiculifolia* (Balkan or spike heath), and *Arctostaphylos uva-ursi*, a member of the heath family, native to the Cape Cod area, which makes an attractive ground cover in sandy places.

Rock Spray also grows a select group of native perennials, such as bearberry, beach plum, rosa rugosa, and bayberry.

"No other group of plants," Herrick says, "can offer so much to the garden as heathers. With proper selection, it is possible to have flowers twelve months of the year, also the contrasting and ever-changing foliage hues can be breathtaking! Add to this the excellent groundcovering effect achieved when planted in masses . . . with proper spacing a solid ever-changing, evergreen tapestry effect can be achieved."

Walden Pond

> I never found the companion
> that was so companionable as solitude.
> **—Henry David Thoreau**

Thoreau, fortunately, can't revisit today's Walden Pond. He'd be hard put to find "solitude" there now. Walden Pond has been named a

State Reservation, and its 411 acres, not too far from Boston, are visited by approximately a million people a year. A warm summer day can bring out thousands.

If you'd like to pay homage to that early naturalist, drive out to Walden Pond. It's open every day from 8 A.M. to sunset. You can go swimming, canoeing, fishing, hiking, and picnicking—but more to Thoreau's liking would be the summer lectures by naturalists and Thoreau scholars.

Walden is on Route 126, ¼ mile south of Route 2. From Route 128, exit west on Route 2. The phone number is (508) 369–3254.

Lyman Estate (The Vale)
185 Lyman St.
Waltham, MA 02154
(617) 891–7095

Open Thurs.–Sun., 10 A.M.–4 P.M.; closed major holidays. Admission fee charged.

From Rte. 95/128 take Rte. 20 (Main St.) through the center of Waltham to Lyman St. and continue to the rotary; turn right into the Lyman estate driveway.

Theodore Lyman, who was a wealthy Boston merchant as well as an enthusiastic horticulturist and gentleman farmer, acquired land for his country estate, "The Vale," in 1793. He planned much of the estate's landscape based on a study of naturalistic English designs. He included thirty acres of "pleasure grounds," which has a 500-foot-long perennial bed.

Four of the five greenhouses on the grounds were built around the early 1800s or before. One of them is believed to be the oldest standing greenhouse in the United States, although it is no longer used.

One of the greenhouses was built for citrus trees, pine-apples, and bananas. Another, the camellia house, reflects Boston's fame as a center for camellia culture during the early 1800s. These were first introduced to the United States in 1797 from their native areas in Asia, and Lyman and his colleagues grew and hybridized them. Many of the trees, which still bloom every year, are over 100 years old.

Annual events that should interest many gardeners are the annual "Camellia Days," when plants propagated from the collection are for sale (February), the plant sale of greenhouse plants (March), the sale of Hamburg and Muscat table grapes (August and September), and the annual Christmas plant sale. Call or write for exact dates.

Cass School of Floral Design

If you're seriously interested in floral design this may be the school for you. A three-week day course or a seven-week evening course will give you a good background in design, construction, and care of plants and flowers along with training in the business side of floral shops, if you're considering becoming a professional.

Subjects include Japanese and European designs, center-pieces, corsages, bridal bouquets, church and temple arrangements, holiday designs, bow making, and dry and silk flower arrangements.

Faith Cass, director of the school, has won numerous awards for floral design throughout the United States, including top awards from the Massachusetts Horticultural Society as well as Gold Medal awards for her displays at flower shows.

The Cass School began as a course for the Massachusetts Horticultural Society in 1981. Since then the school has received national recognition and is now licensed by the Commonwealth of Massachusetts. It is located at 531 Mt. Auburn St., Watertown, MA 02172. Watertown is adjacent to the city of Boston. Call (617) 926-2277 for information.

Botanicals, Inc.   XERIC PERENNIALS
Rte. 126
Wayland, MA 01778
(508) 358–4846   Jeff Louis Licht, Owner

Mail-order sales only; catalog $1. (Display garden may be opened in the future.)

Before Botanicals sells a plant, says Licht, it must meet the following criteria:

- have the ability to withstand some periods of stress
- be mostly cold tolerant
- have attractive flowers and foliage
- be quite unusual and distinctive

Why "xeric," or stress tolerant, plants? Simple, says Licht. "We know that our customers are sophisticated and educated gardeners, that you are already preparing for declining water tables, watering bans, and restrictions. We sure are. As these facts of gardening and landscaping life become more commonplace, low-water-use plants become a smart investment. Further, we continue to discover plants that are fast disappearing from their native habitats, but that, in cultivation, make 'tough,' dependable friends for your woods, meadows, or garden."

Licht has traveled throughout the United States, Europe, and Asia in order to propagate these choice plants, which often come from arboretums and private plant collections.

Few of the over 500 species and cultivars in his inventory are native to New England, but many will do well in New England areas. While only about 120 plants are listed in the Botanicals catalog, if you have specific requirements Licht may be able to fit them in his production schedule.

Categories of the plant material are herbaceous perennials, alpines, forbs and grasses, groundcovers, and shrubs. Several of the plants are summer thistle, a beautiful plant with clusters of pale yellow 1-inch flowers on 1-foot stems, from the mountains of central Europe; the Illinois bundle flower, or prairie mimosa, dense-headed 3-foot plants with whitish flowers, which are becoming rare; and spotted beebalm, a yellow-and-purple flowered beauty that grows aggressively in sandy prairies and open woodlands.

A book that Licht recommends is *The Dry Garden,* by Beth Chatto (J. M. Denton and Sons, Ltd., London, 1978).

This is a very timely subject. Worth looking into.

 Wellesley College—Margaret C. Ferguson Greenhouses, Hunnewell Arboretum, and Alexandra Botanical Garden
Wellesley, MA 02181
(617) 235–0320, ext. 3074

Open every day, 8:30 A.M.–4:30 P.M.

Take Rte. 16 to Wellesley College Campus.

The fifteen greenhouses combined with the 22 acres of the arboretum and botanic gardens are an outstanding teaching facility for Wellesley College and a horticultural resource viewed by thousands each year.

Start your tour at the greenhouses where you can pick up brochures outlining self-guided tours.

The greenhouses have a collection of over 1,000 kinds of plants. Temperature and humidity in each house are controlled independently, providing a range of climates in which plants from all regions of the world grow. Permanent collections include desert plants, tropical plants, orchids, ferns, and many subtropical, temperate, and aquatic plants.

The botanical gardens and arboretum have over 500

species of woody plants in fifty-three families—including lilacs, flowering crabapples and cherries, honeysuckles, hollies, linden trees, Chinese cork trees, and oaks and walnuts.

Guided tours can be arranged; for information about them call (617) 235–0320, ext. 3094, or write Wellesley College Science Center, Wellesley, MA 02181.

Clapper's   GARDEN TOOLS, ACCESSORIES
1125 Washington St.
West Newton, MA 02165
(617) 244–7909   Bob Scagnetti, Owner

Direct retail sales at 1121 Washington St.; open Mon.–Fri., 8 A.M.–5 P.M., Sat., 9 A.M.–12 M. Also mail-order sales; free catalog.

In the greater Boston area; take exit 16 south (Washington St.) off Mass. Tnpk. (I-90); it's next to the Armory.

Clapper's has one of the most extensive lines of quality garden tools available in the Northeast, for example, trowels, saws, grafting knives, many types of pruners and loppers, spades and forks, Cape Cod weeders, dutch hoes, and edgers. Manufacturers include names such as Wilkinson, Felco, Florian, and Corona.

You'll also find soil-testing kits, garden gloves, chippershredders, garden carts, watering cans, sprayers, outdoor lighting equipment, sprinklers, hoses, and a variety of garden ornaments such as sundials, bells, and statuary.

Clapper's has a fairly wide selection of garden furniture including imported English furniture of solid teak and classic American furniture of painted hardwood in kit form. By picking up these and other items at the shop in West Newton you can save a good amount on shipping charges.

🦎 **Case Estates of Arnold Arboretum**
135 Wellesley St.
Weston, MA 02193
(617) 524–1718; (617) 894–0208

Open every day, 9 A.M.–sunset.

From Rte. 128 take exit for Rte. 20 west; go 1 mile on Rte. 20, then turn left on Wellesley St.; Case Estates is 1 mile farther on right.

The Case Estates started out as Hillcrest Gardens, a vegetable and fruit farm, a school for young horticulture students, and a site for plant introductions and display. It was owned by Marion and Louisa Case, who had a longtime interest in horticulture; the Cases bequeathed it to the Arnold Arboretum in the 1940s.

The best way to see the estates is with a self-guided tour, using a map available at the entrance or at the Arnold Arboretum in Jamaica Plain, Massachusetts (see pages 78–80). Among the highlights are a hosta display, a rhododendron grove, herbaceous display beds, a stone wall that is the largest freestanding stone wall in New England, a ground cover and mulch display, a perennial garden, a daylily border, and natural woodlands with paths winding through them.

The general nursery is used for evaluating and testing plants that can later be used at the Arnold Arboretum in Jamaica Plain.

Case Estates offers a number of courses throughout the year. For information about them contact the Arnold Arboretum in Jamaica Plain.

An annual highlight is the Arnold Arboretum's annual plant sale and rare plant auction held at Case Estates in late September. Call for exact date and time.

Nourse Farms, Inc.   STRAWBERRY, OTHER FRUIT AND
River Rd.   VEGETABLE PLANTS
Whately, MA
(Mailing address: RFD, Box 485,
South Deerfield, MA 01373)
(413) 665–2658   Tim Nourse, President

Direct retail sales; open during planting season, Apr. 10–May 20, 8 A.M.–4 P.M. Also mail-order sales; free catalog.

On I-91, north from Northampton, take exit 24 (Deerfield and Amherst); take first right onto Rte. 116 (to Amherst); after 1 mile turn right (south) onto River Rd. at base of Mt. Sugarloaf; the farm is located 3 miles south on River Rd.

Nourse Farms sells plants of strawberries, raspberries, and blackberries; Christmas tree seedlings; horseradish roots; hybrid asparagus crowns; and rhubarb divisions.

Nourse grows all plant stock in its nursery using state-of-the-art tissue culture practices to produce vigorous, virus-free parent stock. (If you're interested in this procedure, write for a free brochure describing the tissue culture program.)

You'll find more than two dozen varieties of strawberries—early, mid-season, and late as well as everbearing varieties, numerous varieties of raspberries, and thorned and thornless blackberries.

Incidentally, if you like fresh-picked raspberries give Nourse Farms a call at the beginning of the raspberry season. They have 10 acres of raspberries—which equals a lot of picking.

Paradise Water Gardens   AQUATIC NURSERIES
14 May St. (Rte. 18)
Whitman, MA 02382
(617) 447–4711   Paul Stetson, Sr., President

Direct retail sales; open Mon.–Fri., year-round, 8 A.M.–6 P.M., Sat., 8 A.M.–5 P.M., Sun., 1 P.M.–5 P.M. Also mail-order sales; catalog $3.

About midway between Boston and Providence, R.I.; from Boston take Rte. 3 south to Rte. 18; continue south to Whitman; or take Rte. 495 south to Rte. 18; then go north on Rte. 18 to Whitman.

Paradise Water Gardens was founded by Paul Stetson, Sr., who has been raising water lilies since he was a boy. "Years ago," he says, "only the wealthy could afford a water garden. Now anyone can make a showplace in his or her backyard for a minimal cost. A small pool can cost as little as fifty dollars."

However, don't plan to get away with only $50 if you're interested in water gardening and visit Paradise Gardens. You'll be lured by exotic water lilies, Japanese iris, lotus blossoms, fancy goldfish and koi, fiberglass pools in just about every shape you can dream up, waterfalls, cascades, streams, fountains, underwater lights, Japanese lanterns and statuary, and on and on.

The company manufactures a large percentage of its own products, thus keeping costs lower, produces its own water lilies and aquatic plants (after the hardy water lilies go through the rigors of New England winters they adapt well to all climates), and raises many of its own fish.

The gardens are at their best from mid-May on, when aquatic plants and water lilies reach maturity, but are worth a visit at any time—especially if you're interested in things aquatic.

As Stetson says, "We provide *everything* you need for water gardens."

Allgrove Farm, Inc.   TERRARIUM PLANTS, SUPPLIES
P.O. Box 459
Wilmington, MA 01887
(508) 658–4869   Warren B. Allgrove, President

Direct retail sales by appointment only. (Get directions when calling.) Mail-order sales; catalog 50 cents.

Begun in 1932 by the late Arthur Eames Allgrove to provide "nostalgic New England plants for woodsy dish gardens, terrariums, bonsai, and the wildflower garden," the nursery is now run by his family, continuing in the same tradition.

Terrarium plants available include partridge berry, rattlesnake plantain, trailing arbutus, ebony spleenwort, shining club moss, walking fern, striped pipsissewa, goldthread, shinleaf, round lobe hepatica, northern pitcher plant, British soldier, fairy caps, and more.

Allgrove has an assortment of mosses, fungi, and lichen, featherrock, bowls in several sizes, and kits for partridge berry bowls and wreaths. The nursery also has a number of terrarium kits, including sizes for garden clubs and other groups, designed for twenty or more participants.

Mahoney's Rocky Ledge Farm & Nursery*

COMPLETE GARDEN CENTER

242 Cambridge St.
Winchester, MA 01890
(617) 729–5900

Paul J. Mahoney, Owner

Direct retail sales; open every day, year-round, 9 A.M.–6 P.M.; stays open later in spring and before Christmas.

Take exit 33A off Rte. 128 south; go 3 miles south on Rte. 3 to nursery.

*Mahoney's also has two other locations: Mahoney's Too Tewksbury, 1609 Main St. (Rte. 38) in Tewksbury and Mahoney's Too East Falmouth, 958 Main St. (Rte. 28) in East Falmouth.

All locations have the same hours and also the same phone number: (617) 729–5900.

When you get to Mahoney's be sure to pick up a map. Without one you could well get lost (you may, even with one). Mahoney's lays claim to being the largest retail nursery and garden center in the Northeast.

Among the shopping areas you can browse through are the South Greenhouse, the North Greenhouse, a perennials display, an annuals plot, rose plots, a florist and gift ship, the barn, two information booths (if you get lost or want horticultural advice), the Main Gate (thousands of shrubs, evergreens, vines, trees, Christmas trees in season), the Farm Stand (edibles), and the Front Garden (to inspire you).

The map has an alphabetical list on the back that tells you where to go for what, such as baskets (South Greenhouse), bonsai (North Greenhouse), fruit-bearing shrubs (the Main Gate), grass seed (the Barn), maple syrup (the Farm Stand), vines (outside the North Greenhouse), and topsoil (the Main Gate).

Despite its size, Paul J. Mahoney, who has been the sole owner since 1959, adds a personal touch. He still insists on selecting all the shrubs himself—as he's done for more than twenty-five years.

New Hampshire

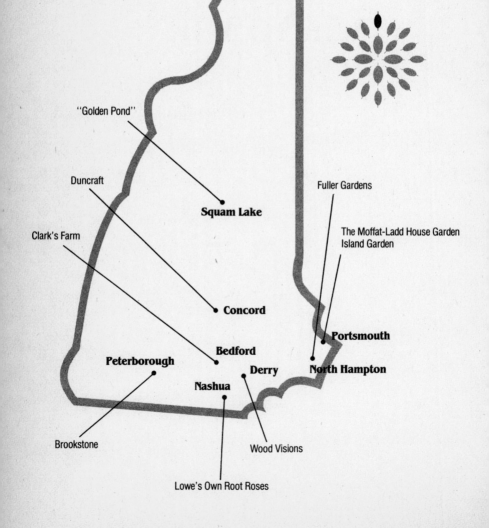

NEW HAMPSHIRE

"Golden Pond"

Duncraft

Clark's Farm

Squam Lake

Fuller Gardens

The Moffat-Ladd House Garden
Island Garden

Concord

Portsmouth

Bedford

Peterborough

Derry

North Hampton

Nashua

Brookstone

Wood Visions

Lowe's Own Root Roses

Clark's Farm   FLOWER AND VEGETABLE PLANTS, MUMS
111 Worthley Rd.
Bedford, NH 03102
(603) 623-9567   Richard Clark, Jr., Owner

Direct retail sales; greenhouses and farm stand open Mon.–Sat., 9 A.M.–6 P.M., Sun., 9 A.M.–5:30 P.M.

In Bedford take Rte. 114 north to Bedford Rd. to Rundlett Rd., go north to Worthley Rd.

Richard Clark, Jr., has been operating Clark's Farm since 1961 and now grows over 1,200 varieties of plants from seed. Fifty acres are devoted to producing annuals, perennials, and vegetables, with plants available in spring and produce in summer.

But probably of most interest to gardeners are the fall hardy mums for which Clark's is famous. The exceptional combinations of size, balance, and bud count have captured fifty-one blue ribbons and draw customers from around the Northeast. Clark grows the mums from seed and does much work in developing new varieties and growing methods. And he's available to give personal help to buyers with problems and questions.

Duncraft   WILD BIRD SUPPLIES
Rte. 3, Concord, NH 03301
(Mailing address: Penacook, NH 03303)
(603) 224–0200   Mike Dunn, Owner

Direct retail sales at factory store, Concord, N.H.; open Mon.–Sat., 9 A.M.–5 P.M. Also mail-order sales; write for free catalog.

From Concord take Rte. 3, 4 miles north to factory store.

Duncraft has many types of bird feeders (including designs especially for small birds), purple martin houses, a gourmet selection of seeds and suet, heaters for birdbaths, whistles for producing bird calls, videocassettes showing over 200 species with closeups of fifty-two birds, records and cassettes of bird songs, field guides to birds, and one-way mirror film for putting on a window so you can see birds outside up close enough to count their whiskers—without the birds being able to see you. In other words, just about everything to make a birder happy.

The majority of Duncraft's business is mail order but the factory store sells items listed in the catalog as well as manufacturing seconds, overstocks, and samples.

Wood Visions   GAZEBOS
P.O. Box 815
Derry, NH 03038
(603) 437–9663   David M. Rugh, Owner

Direct retail sales; open by appointment. Also mail-order sales; write for free catalog.

Take Rte. 93 north from Boston to N.H. exit 5; go right off exit for 2 miles; the shop is on the right.

Wood Visions makes modular gazebos in kit form, crafted from clear, western red cedar. Rugh says they are "top of the line, constructed from finest materials and built to last for years." The structures have brass-threaded connecting hardware for assembly, prewired electrical service, and cedar-shingled roof panels.

The gazebos are designed to sit on a concrete foundation and can be assembled by two people in one day. The only tool needed is a set of socket wrenches, along with a ladder. All work is done from ground level or from the gazebo floor.

Because of western red cedar's high resistance to decay no application of a liquid finish is required and the gazebo will turn to a pleasing light gray tone. Options are available for hot tubs, screening, bench and table arrangements, and ramps. Or the gazebo can be completely custom designed. Prices start at a little over $4,000.

If you're interested in Wood Visions's gazebos, it may be well worth your time to drive to Derry. You can see gazebos displayed in the manufacturing plant as well as seeing completed installations.

A Side Trip to Golden Pond?

Sorry, there is no Golden Pond. But if you'd like to see the lake where that memorable 1980 movie, starring Katharine Hepburn and Henry Fonda, was made take a short detour from Route 93 in central New Hampshire. On Route 3, near Ashland and northwest of Lake Winnipesaukee, is Squam Lake—the mythical Golden Pond.

Keep in mind, however, that if you'd like to swim in the lake, canoe on it, rent a cottage near it, or even buy some land around it, the answer is no—as many disappointed people learned soon after the movie was released. Squam Lake is very secluded and private and peaceful and the people who live there aim to keep it that way.

Lowe's Own Root Roses

ROOTED ROSES

6 Sheffield Rd.
Nashua, NH 03062
(603) 888–2214 (from mid-May–mid-Oct.,
call before 3 P.M. or after 8 P.M.)

Malcolm Lowe,
Owner

Rose display garden with 4,000 bushes, 700 varieties, open by appointment. Sales by mail order; catalog $2.

Take Rte. 3 from Mass. to exit 4 in N.H.; go west on E. Dunstable Rd., then right on New Searles Rd.; go to the end and turn right onto Searles; take the second left, at Sheffield to the nursery.

Malcolm "Mike" Lowe, a certified rose judge with the American
Rose Society, describes his rose growing as a "labor of love."
(He's also an engineer with Raytheon.)

His main interest is preserving and reintroducing old
garden roses. Many of his varieties come from Peter Beales and
David Austin in England, Wilhelm Kordes in Germany, Ellen
and Hugo Lykke in Denmark, and the private collections of
Leonie Bell and Karl Jones and others in the United States. He
also has access to the species rose collection in the Arnold Arboretum in Boston.

Orders must be placed by May 1 each year, so that cuttings to be rooted can be taken in May. They are ready about
October 30 of the following year—eighteen months later. Plants
can be picked up at the nursery at that time and occasionally
surplus plants are available then.

Lowe holds an open house in late June; call for the exact
date. He's also available to give lectures with color slides on all
aspects of old and modern roses.

Fuller Gardens

10 Willow Ave.
North Hampton, NH 03862
(603) 964–5414

Open every day, end of May–Labor Day, 10 A.M.–6 P.M. Admission fee charged.

Take Rte. I-95 to Rte. 101-D (Atlantic Ave.); go east to Rte. 1-A; the
gardens are 200 yards north of the junction of 101-D and 1-A.

Fuller Gardens, the estate of the late Governor Alvan Fuller, is
a seaside gem. The 2-acre garden has many features that make
it one of New England's finest public gardens.

The gardens feature extensive plantings of roses, ac-
cented by fountains and statuary and a dazzling ocean back-

ground. Other features are a Japanese garden, a wildflower walk, perennial borders, and beds of colorful annuals. The conservatory contains a collection of exotic tropical and desert plants.

The gardens change by the season. In the spring you'll see masses of tulips, wildflowers, and azaleas and rhododendrons. In late June, hundreds of roses begin a display that continues nonstop through October. Colors in the perennial borders continue throughout the season, and brilliant beds of chrysanthemums highlight the fall.

Two special gardens of interest are the official All-America Rose Selections display garden for New Hampshire, and the All-America award-winning annuals garden; in each you can see the prize winners of recent years.

A plant sale is held in early May, and several garden seminars take place in the summer. Call or write for exact dates.

Highly recommended.

Brookstone   GARDEN TOOLS
Vose Farm Rd.
Peterborough, NH 03458
(603) 924–7181   Henry Lee, Vice President

Direct retail sales; open Mon.–Fri. 9:30 A.M.–5 P.M. Brookstone has a number of other retail stores throughout New England; see below. Also mail-order sales; write for free catalog.

The Peterborough store is just off Rte. 202 north, above Peterborough and opposite Conval High School on the east side of Rte. 202.

Brookstone, whose products are described as "hard-to-find tools," has been selling garden tools for about twenty years (along with many other items). Henry Lee says the company emphasizes quality of design, workmanship, and materials *and* makes sure products are environmentally safe.

Among recent offerings are the garden trike, a tractor-

like seat mounted on three wheels just 15 inches high so you
don't have to bend or stoop to work in the garden; plant ties
made of foam-coated wire, which won't injure delicate stems or
branches; a conversion kit for an electric drill that can be used
to start most engines with rope-pull starters; planters that look
like wood but are made of fiberglass and will last forever or so;
fierce-looking owls that scare birds and rodents away from gardens; and—sounds too good to be true—a weeder whose weight,
balance, and length give you the same feeling as swinging a golf
club and will eradicate weeds and at the same time strengthen
your wrists and forearms.

Other Brookstone stores, usually in shopping malls, in
the Northeast are

Copley Place, Marketplace Center and 29 School St., in
Boston

South Shore Plaza, Braintree, Massachusetts

The Mall of New Hampshire, Manchester, New Hampshire

Pheasant Lane Mall, Nashua, New Hampshire

Crossgates Mall, Albany, New York

Herald Center and South Street Seaport in New York
City

Stamford Town Center, Stamford, Connecticut

Crystal Mall, Waterford, Connecticut

Westfarms Mall, West Hartford, Connecticut

For information about hours and exact location of these
stores, call Brookstone in Peterborough at (603) 924–9511.

The Moffatt-Ladd House Garden

154 Market St.
Portsmouth, NH 03801
(603) 436-8221

Open Mon.–Sat., June 15–Oct. 15, 10 A.M.–4 P.M., Sun, 2 P.M.–
5 P.M. Admission fee charged.

Going north on I-95, take Portsmouth exit 7, to Market St.

The Moffatt-Ladd House was built in 1763 by John Moffatt as
a wedding gift for his son and was occupied by his descendants
until 1900. In 1912 the property was entrusted to the Colonial
Dames of America in New Hampshire.

No large colonial house in Portsmouth was without a
garden, and the garden here occupies about 1½ acres, entirely
enclosed by the house, paneled wood fences, and borders of
lilacs, creating a secluded area in the city.

A series of four terraces behind the house, leading to a
gate at the rear of the property, make up the formal garden.
Flower beds are separated by lawn; brick and gravel paths are
raised to various heights by terracing.

A winding path leads along the north side of the garden,
among shrubs and fruit trees—two of which still produce a good
crop of pears. Other features of the garden include a spiral
trellis of old Portsmouth design, an herb garden, and a damask
rose brought from England by the first bride. On the east side
of the house is an enormous horse-chestnut tree planted by John
Moffatt's son-in-law on his return from signing the Declaration
of Independence in 1776. Flowers, including a great many perennials, annuals, and bulbs, are heirloom varieties, reflecting
gardens of this early period.

An annual candlelight tour of six old houses in the Portsmouth area of Strawberry Banke is held each August. And you
can rent the Moffatt-Ladd House Garden for special func-
tions—weddings, garden parties, dinners, etc. Call or write for
information.

Visit Celia Thaxter's Island Garden

If you've enjoyed the book *An Island Garden,* by Celia Thaxter, a trip to her island should be a priority. If you haven't yet read her book, get a copy and do so. Houghton Mifflin has published a faithful reproduction of that 1894 classic, including the original watercolors by Childe Hassam.

Lying about 6 miles off the New Hampshire coast, 95-acre Appledore Island is the largest of the nine Isles of Shoals. During the late nineteenth century a resort hotel on Appledore drew many noteworthy members of the American art, poetry, writing, and music world. Among them were Nathaniel Hawthorne, Harriet Beecher Stowe, John Greenleaf Whittier, Sarah Orne Jewett, and artist Childe Hassam. Celia Thaxter was the hostess of the hotel and her passion was creating a formal garden on the island, which she immortalized in her book.

In 1914 the Appledore House Hotel burned to the ground and was never rebuilt. Since then Appledore has become quite isolated. But recently the Shoals Marine Laboratory, sponsored by the University of New Hampshire and Cornell University, has had summer programs on the island. And with access to the island available, Virginia P. Chisholm, Chairman of the Moffatt-Ladd House Garden in Portsmouth (see pages 118–119), with the help of volunteers, has restored Celia's island garden to the way it was planted in 1893. (And her results were highlighted on Charles Kuralt's *CBS Sunday Morning* show.)

To reach Appledore visitors take the scheduled ferry service from Portsmouth, New Hampshire, to the Isles of Shoals. The ferry runs from mid-June to the beginning of September and docks at Star Island. Although there's no regular ferry service to Appledore, a vessel from the Shoals Marine laboratory provides service from Star Island to Appledore for $2. Arrangements for the ferry should be made in advance; this can be done by calling (607) 255–3717— the Shoals Marine laboratory offices at Cornell. (Even though this is an out-of-state call, arrangements can be made very quickly.)

This can make a very fascinating day's trip. In addition to Celia's garden, you can explore the island. Whales are usually sighted on every trip, porpoises and dolphins visit the area each year, and a colony of harbor seals breeds nearby. The island has a heron

rookery and the Audubon Society and other bird clubs make pil-
grimages to it every summer.

The Isles of Shoals are on the National Register of Historic
Places.

— New York

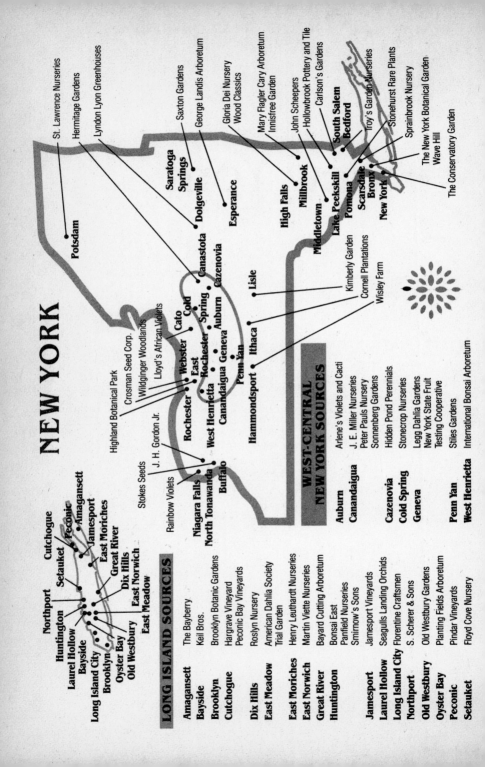

NEW YORK

St. Lawrence Nurseries
Hermitage Gardens
Lyndon Lyon Greenhouses
Potsdam

Saxton Gardens
George Landis Arboretum
Gloria Dei Nursery
Wood Classics
Mary Flagler Cary Arboretum
Innistree Garden
John Scheepers
Hollowbrook Pottery and Tile
Carlson's Gardens
Troy's Garden Nurseries
Stonehurst Rare Plants
Sprainbrook Nursery
The New York Botanical Garden
Wave Hill
The Conservatory Garden

Saratoga
Springs
Dolgeville
Esperance
High Falls
Millbrook
Middletown
Lake Peekskill
Pomona
Scarsdale
Bronx
New York
South Salem
Bedford

Canastota
Cazenovia
Liste
Cold
Spring
Auburn
Penn Yan
Ithaca
Kimberly Garden
Cornell Plantations
Wisley Farm

Webster
East
Cato
Rochester
Geneva
Hammondsport

Crosman Seed Corp.
Wildginger Woodlands
Lloyd's African Violets
Highland Botanical Park
J. H. Gordon Jr.

Rochester
West Henrietta
Canandaigua

Stokes Seeds
Rainbow Violets
Niagara Falls
North Tonawanda
Buffalo

WEST-CENTRAL NEW YORK SOURCES

Auburn	Arlene's Violets and Cacti
Canandaigua	J. E. Miller Nurseries
	Peter Pauls Nursery
	Sonnenberg Gardens
Cazenovia	Hidden Pond Perennials
Cold Spring	Stonecrop Nurseries
Geneva	Legg Dahlia Gardens
	New York State Fruit
	Testing Cooperative
Penn Yan	Stiles Gardens
West Henrietta	International Bonsai Arboretum

LONG ISLAND SOURCES

Amagansett	The Bayberry
Bayside	Keil Bros.
Brooklyn	Brooklyn Botanic Gardens
Cutchogue	Hargrave Vineyard
	Peconic Bay Vineyards
Dix Hills	Roslyn Nursery
East Meadow	American Dahlia Society
	Trial Garden
East Moriches	Henry Leuthardt Nurseries
East Norwich	Martin Viette Nurseries
Great River	Bayard Cutting Arboretum
Huntington	Bonsai East
	Panfield Nurseries
	Smirnow's Sons
Jamesport	Jamesport Vineyards
Laurel Hollow	Seagulls Landing Orchids
Long Island City	Florentine Craftsmen
Northport	S. Scherer & Sons
Old Westbury	Old Westbury Gardens
	Planting Fields Arboretum
Peconic	Pindar Vineyards
Setauket	Floyd Cove Nursery

Northport
Huntington
Laurel Hollow
Bayside
Brooklyn
Long Island City
Oyster Bay
Old Westbury
Setauket
Cutchogue
Peconic
Amagansett
Jamesport
East River
Great River
Dix Hills
East Norwich
East Meadow

The Bayberry, Inc.
Montauk Hwy.
Amagansett, NY 11930
(Mailing address: Box 718,
Amagansett, NY 11930)
(516) 267–3000

RARE TREES AND SHRUBS,
GARDEN ACCESSORIES

David E. Seeler, President

Direct retail sales; open every day, Apr. 1–Nov. 1, 8 A.M.–4:30 P.M. Also mail-order sales; write for brochure.

On Montauk Hwy.; 2 miles east of East Hampton.

The Bayberry specializes in rare and dwarf trees and shrubs and also features perennials and ornamental grasses. The 10-acre garden showroom has an arboretum, a May–June garden, a July–August garden, a wildflower garden, and beds of annuals. The numerous accessories include teak and redwood furniture, copper weather vanes, lanterns, sun umbrellas, dovecotes, and fountains and all are displayed in garden settings.

Customers are in capable hands. The Bayberry has a staff of sixty and all salespeople have degrees in horticulture or landscape architecture.

Arlene's Violets and Cacti
33 Frazee St.
Auburn, NY 13021
(315) 252–6218

AFRICAN VIOLETS, RELATED
GESNERIADS, CACTI

Arlene B. Alexander, Owner

Direct retail sales only; open most of the time; call ahead to verify.

Take the N.Y. Thruway to Rte. 34; go south to Auburn; further directions are given when you call.

Alexander has a large selection of both older and the latest varieties of standard, mini, and trailing African violets, along with other gesneriads, from leading hybridizers in the United States and Canada. Also a good selection of cactus plants. She has many planters in stock, including self-watering types, and numerous growing supplies.

Active in the plant world, Alexander belongs to a number of organizations, including the African Violet Society of America, the Gesneriad Society International, the New York State African Violet Society, and the African Violet Society of Canada.

Keil Bros., Inc.   NURSERY STOCK, GARDEN
220-15 Horace Harding Blvd.   SUPPLIES, TROPICAL PLANTS
Bayside, NY 11364
(718) 224—2020   Ronald and Richard Keil

Direct retail sales only; open every day, 8:30 A.M.—5 P.M.; longer hours during seasonal periods.

Long Island Expwy. (Rte. 495) to exit 29.

Henry Keil got his start by selling cut flowers on a street corner in 1930. This wouldn't seem to be the best time—with the country in a depression—to begin selling what might be considered a luxury item. But using his business acumen, Keil had chosen a corner opposite a country club golf course in Bayside, and his sales were excellent as well-to-do golfers stopped to buy on their way home.

Today Keil Bros. is on the same street corner, in a complex of greenhouses and a garden center, although the country club has long since given way to housing developments and the Long Island Expressway is at its door. The company is now a corporation with Keil's sons and son-in-law as officers. A nursery and growing operation is located in Bohemia, Long Island.

In addition to general nursery stock, Keil Bros. sells heaths and heathers, rock garden plants, and other perennials. Tropical plants are available in the greenhouse, and the garden center is well stocked with garden supplies, including power tools and equipment, fertilizers, pesticides, and topsoil. In season, Christmas trees, wreaths, and holiday decorations are major items.

Troy's Garden Nurseries, Inc.   GENERAL NURSERY
Greenwich Rd.   STOCK
Bedford, NY 10506
(914) 234–3400   John H. Troy II, President

Direct retail sales; open Mon.–Fri., Jan.–mid-Mar., 9 A.M.–4:30 P.M.; mid-Mar.–June, also open Sat., 10 A.M.–5 P.M., Sun. 11 A.M.–4 P.M.; Mon.–Fri., July–Aug., 8 A.M.–5 P.M., Sat., 10 A.M.–5 P.M.; Mon.– Fri., Sept.–Dec., 8 A.M.–5 P.M., Sat., 10 A.M.–5 P.M., Sun., 10 A.M.–4 P.M.

Greenwich Rd. is the main road between Bedford, N.Y., and Greenwich, Conn. It can be reached either by the Merritt Pkwy. or Rte. 684 to Rte. 22.

Troy's Garden Nurseries has been taking care of the area's gardeners since 1887 when it was begun by the first John H. Troy. There's a tremendous amount of background experience here for gardeners to call on.

Troy's makes both retail and wholesale sales. Among its specialties are a large selection of rare and unusual evergreens and trees, and outstanding perennial and daylily varieties. Do-it-yourself, or if you prefer, take it easy and Troy's will provide complete landscaping services from design to finish.

During the Christmas season you can visit the Christmas shop for trees, wreaths, roping, and seasonal plants.

 The New York Botanical Garden
200th St. & Southern Blvd.
Bronx, NY 10458
(212) 220–8700

Grounds open Tues.–Sun., Apr.–Oct., 8 A.M.–7 P.M.; Tues.–Sun., Nov.–Mar., 8 A.M.–6 P.M.; conservatory open Tues.–Sun., 10 A.M.–4 P.M.; closed Christmas and New Year's Day. Admission to grounds, voluntary fee. Fee charged for admission to conservatory.

Take the Bronx River Pkwy. to Rte. 1. Go west to Southern Blvd.

The New York Botanical Garden is not something you can "do in a day." You could visit it over a lifetime and find something new each trip.

These 250 acres of nature draw over a million visitors each year and include 40 acres of natural forest—the only uncut stand of forest in New York City. The Bronx River enters the garden at its northern edge, by the Twin Lakes, winds through the forest, spills over the Snuff Mill dam, then leaves the garden at the Bronx Zoo.

Among the many special gardens are the rose garden, with more than 200 varieties of roses; the Jane Watson Irwin Garden, which has a great variety of perennials, ornamental grasses, and bulbs, and a background of over 100 species of clematis; the herb garden; the rock garden; the native plant garden; and the demonstration gardens, which display ideas on designs and plants appropriate for the house and apartment.

The grounds have many azaleas and rhododendrons, a Japanese flowering cherry collection, a crabapple and magnolia collection, and a conifer collection.

The Enid A. Haupt Conservatory, consisting of eleven glasshouses around a rectangular courtyard and covering 44,000 square feet, is probably the highlight of the garden. It houses many permanent collections, outstanding specimen plants, and changing seasonal displays of flowers. Among the presentations are Gardens of the Past, the Greenworld for Children, the New World Desert, the Fern Forest, and Tropical Flora.

The New York Botanical Garden (NYBG) sponsors many educational programs and research projects. Courses range from college level to one-day workshops. In addition to programs at the Bronx campus, the NYBG sponsors courses at four satellite centers in Ridgewood, New Jersey, in New Canaan, Connecticut, at the Queens Botanical Garden in Flushing, New York, and at the Horticultural Society of New York. For more information about these write for a copy of the current course catalog. NYBG also conducts ecosystem research at the Mary Flagler Cary Arboretum in Millbrook, New York (see pages 158– 159).

Wave Hill
675 W. 252d St.
Bronx, NY 10471
(212) 549–3200

Open every day 10 A.M.–4:30 P.M.; closed Christmas Day and New Year's Day; extended hours between Memorial Day and Labor Day. Admission fee charged weekends only.

Northbound on the Henry Hudson Pkwy.: exit at 246th St. Go on service rd. to 252d St., then turn left over the pkwy. and turn left again. Go right at 249th St. to Wave Hill gate. Southbound on the Henry Hudson Pkwy.: exit at 254th St.; take an immediate left at stop sign and left again at light. Go south to 249th St., then turn right and go to Wave Hill gate.

Wave Hill is a public garden on 28 acres overlooking the Hudson River. Besides two manor houses built in the 1800s the grounds have two greenhouses, an English-style wild garden, an herb garden, an old-fashioned flower garden, a monocot garden, and an aquatic garden.

Greenhouse and garden walks are held every Sunday at 2:15 P.M. A number of horticultural activities are planned throughout the year; these include lectures, slide shows, winter botany walks, demonstrations of maple sugaring, and exploring the Hudson Valley as it was in the Ice Age and the postglacial period.

A number of concerts, art exhibitions, and dance programs are also offered throughout the year. Call or write Wave Hill to get a schedule of activities.

 Brooklyn Botanic Garden
1000 Washington Ave.
Brooklyn, NY 11225
(718) 622–4433

Open Tues.–Fri., Apr.–Sept., 8 A.M.–6 P.M., weekends and holidays, 10 A.M.–6 P.M.; Tues.–Fri., Oct.–Mar., 8 A.M.–4:30 P.M., weekends and holidays, 10 A.M.–4:30 P.M.; closed Mon. unless public holiday falls on that day. No admission fee for grounds; admission fee charged for conservatory.

From the Brooklyn-Queens Expwy. exit onto Atlantic Ave., then turn right onto Washington Ave.

The 52 acres of the Brooklyn Botanic Garden (BBG) make up an oasis in the midst of a city for the hundreds of thousands of visitors who go there every year. In the summer, when the gardens change constantly, some people make it a point to visit almost daily.

The horticultural collection, or the gardens within a garden, include the Rose Garden, with the third-largest public collection of roses on display in the United States; the Fragrance Garden, especially enjoyed by the visually impaired; the Japanese Hill and Pond Garden, which is considered the finest of its kind outside of Japan; the Herb Garden, centered around an Elizabethan knot; the Shakespeare Garden; and the Children's Garden, in operation since 1914 and which has become the prototype for children's gardens around the world.

About half of the garden's acreage is devoted to the systematic collection—trees, shrubs, and herbaceous plants are scientifically arranged by families, with the more primitive plants, such as ferns and conifers, located in the center and the remainder divided into main subclasses of flowering plants.

The Steinhardt Conservatory, completed recently, is a complex of a long rectangular greenhouse and three octagonal pavilions. It greatly expands the area for the BBG's indoor plant collection. Included in it are a jungle rain forest in the Tropical Pavilion; the Temperate Pavilion; the Desert Pavilion; the Bonsai Museum, with the largest bonsai collection in the United States; an Aquatic Greenhouse, with tropical water plants in fresh water and bog pools; and collections of orchids, houseplants, and insectivorous plants.

One of the outstanding features of the BBG is its menu of educational programs. Workshops, lectures, tours, and classes are available for children and adults. (Favorite topics for adults include herbs and bonsai.) In addition, the BBG has an extensive horticultural library, an herbarium of 250,000 dried plant specimens, and free plant information service by phone and mail.

The garden publishes the popular *Plants & Gardens Handbook* series of over sixty titles, which are sold in garden centers throughout the country. There is also a garden shop that sells plants, containers, tools, books, and posters.

Well-attended annual events are benefit plant sales held the first Wednesday and Thursday in May and in the fall on election day.

Visit Stokes Seed Farms and Proving Grounds

Stokes Seeds doesn't have a retail store. Sales are made only through their catalog (to get a free copy, write Stokes Seeds Inc., Box 548, Buffalo, NY 14240). But you're invited to join the hundreds of visitors who come each year to see the 3 acres of vegetable and flower trial gardens and 150 acres of seed crops in St. Catharines, Ontario. The gardens are open from 8 A.M. to 8 P.M., seven days a week.

From Niagara Falls take Queen Elizabeth Way to the city of St. Catharines (which is 30 miles from Buffalo, New York) to the Martindale Road exit; then continue north to the farm. The U.S. phone number is (416) 688–4300.

Stokes sells over 1,600 varieties of vegetable and flower seeds and each year supplies some 38,000 commercial growers and more than 200,000 home gardeners with seeds.

J. E. Miller Nurseries, Inc.   FRUIT TREES, GENERAL
5060 W. Lake Rd.   NURSERY STOCK
Canandaigua, NY 14424
(716) 396–2647   John E. Miller, President

Direct retail sales; nursery and store open every day, mid-Mar.–June 1, 8 A.M.–4:30 P.M.; Mon.–Fri., June 1–mid-Mar., 8 A.M.–4:30 P.M.; closed weekends. Also mail-order sales; free catalog.

Take exit 44 on N.Y. Thruway to Canandaigua, then go south 8 miles on W. Lake Rd.; the nurseries are well marked in Canandaigua.

Miller Nurseries was founded in 1878 by John E. Miller's great-grandfather. The Canandaigua climate then, as today, says the current Miller, tested growing things with a vengeance.

"Throughout a century plus," he says, "we Millers learned which plants would thrive in our rigorous climate, and which to avoid."

The plants that thrive—and only those—are the ones that are sold. Among fruits offered are pears, apples, currants, kiwis, apricots, cherries, peaches, nectarines, blueberries, grapes, and raspberries. You'll also find nut trees, roses, and general nursery stock.

Peter Pauls Nursery   CARNIVOROUS AND TERRARIUM
Chapin Rd.   PLANTS
Canandaigua, NY 14424
(716) 394–7397   James Pietropaolo, Manager

> Mail-order sales; write for free brochure.

Peter Pauls has been selling carnivorous plants since 1957 and
has a sizable collection. Some of them include terrestrial blad-
derworts (from the United States, South America, Africa, and
Australia), rare varieties of *Drosera*, butterworts, sundews, pitcher
plants (from both California and Australia), and Venus flytraps.
The nursery also has an assortment of seeds, kits of woodland
terrarium plants, and terrariums.

"The best advice I can give," says Pietropaolo, "is to read
about the cultural requirements of carnivorous plants before
buying them."

If you want to do this in depth, read *Carnivorous Plants
of the World,* by James and Patricia Pietropaolo. The book has
230 pages, 55 color photographs, and many line drawings. It
covers just about everything you need to know to successfully
grow, propagate, and enjoy carnivorous plants. Price is $30
postpaid in the United States, $32 postpaid to all other coun-
tries.

Sonnenberg Gardens
151 Charlotte St.
Canandaigua, NY 14424
(Mailing address: P.O. Box 663, Canandaigua, NY 14424)
(716) 394–4922

Open every day, mid-May–mid-Oct., 9:30 A.M.–5:30 P.M. Admission fee charged.

*From N.Y. Thruway take exit 44 to Rte. 332 (Main St.) to Canan-
daigua; continue on Main St. to Gibson St., then go east to Charlotte;
turn left (north) to Sonnenberg Gardens.*

Sonnenberg (German for "sunny hill") Gardens are well worth a visit, says the Smithsonian Institution, which described them as "one of the most magnificent late Victorian gardens ever created in America." Sonnenberg was the summer home of Frederick Ferris Thompson, founder of the First National City Bank of New York.

Here are some of the highlights.

The Reflecting Pond
Surrounded by unique specimen trees, it was designed to reflect the forty-room stone mansion on the estate.

The Japanese Garden
It's a classic hill garden, with each stone and plant placed in accordance with ancient rules, graced by a teahouse.

The Sub Rosa Garden
Also called the Secret Garden, it is in a secluded chapel-like setting with plantings of green and white.

The Rose Garden
Over 4,000 rose bushes from the former Jackson and Perkins Rose Gardens in Newark, New York, are planted here, in a design of intersecting circles.

The Blue and White Garden
All the flowers growing here are blue or white.

The Colonial Garden
This geometric garden has over ¼ mile of low box hedges forming a pattern of five circles.

The Rock Garden
It includes 500 feet of streams, waterfalls, and pools fed by geysers and simulated springs hidden in grottos.

The Conservatory
In addition to tropical plants, it houses two gift shops (garden and Victorian), a restaurant, and a wine-tasting room.

Annual events include Rose Sunday and a holiday open house. Call or write for scheduled dates.

Hermitage Gardens   DECORATIVE WATER GARDENS

W. Seneca Ave. (N.Y. Rte. 5)
Canastota, NY 13032
(Mailing address: P.O. Box 361,
Canastota, NY 13032)
(315) 697–9093   Russell A. Rielle, Owner

Direct retail sales; open Mon.–Sat., year-round, 8 A.M.–5 P.M.; Sun., 12 M.–5 P.M., except Jan.–Feb. Also mail-order sales; send $1 for catalog.

Take exit 34 on N.Y. Thruway, go left to third light; turn right and go ½ mile, then turn left on N.Y. Rte. 5 (W. Seneca Ave.); the garden center is across from the Canastota Airport.

Hermitage Gardens manufactures and sells fiberglass garden pools in square, round, oval, rectangular, and free-form shapes; fiberglass "rock" waterfalls and streams; waterwheels (up to 10 feet in diameter); bridges; "Bubbling Fantasias," which combine light and water movement; fountains; lights; pumps; and accessories.

Making a water garden by joining various pools and streams together and adding bridges, waterfalls, etc., can be a do-it-yourself project, says Hermitage Gardens. You can cut the fiberglass components and then join and glue them together with fiberglass paste and hardener; the company provides full directions.

Hermitage, however, specializes in designing waterscaping systems, ranging from those for private homes to shopping centers, office buildings, and malls and has a crew to make the installations. Among others, Hermitage has done several Japanese gardens priced at up to $60,000. (The majority of projects, however, Rielle hastens to add, are much less expensive.)

Hermitage Gardens was founded by Russell A. Rielle in 1946 and is the oldest landscape company in central New York. Among Rielle's credentials are the recommendations his landscaping has received from the Brooklyn Botanic Gardens.

Lloyd's African Violets   AFRICAN VIOLETS
2568 E. Main St.
Cato, NY 13033
(315) 626–2314   JoAnn Lloyd, Owner-Grower

Direct retail sales; open every day, 9 A.M.–5 P.M., but suggest a call first. Also mail-order sale of leaves; send stamp for free list.

Take N.Y. Thruway east from Syracuse; take exit 40, go 8 miles north to Cato; then go right at the stoplight in the village; Lloyd's is located one-half block from the light on the right side of street; it is a dark brown house; a sign is in the front yard.

Lloyd started her business in 1976, specializing in African violets. She sells starter plants, gift plants in various sizes, trailers in hanging baskets, leaves, pots, fertilizers, and other supplies.

She has dozens of varieties from leading hybridizers in the United States and Canada. Visitors are always welcome but Lloyd suggests calling first to make sure she's in. And she says she will gladly help anyone with violet problems.

Lloyd is well qualified to do this. Along with all her growing experience she's an active member and director of the African violet societies of New York, Rochester, and Canada; the Nutmeg State and the Bay State African violet societies; and the American Gloxinia and Gesneriad Society.

Hidden Pond Perennials   PERENNIALS
3699 Rippleton Rd.
Cazenovia, NY 13035
(315) 655–8754   Nancy E. Hook, Owner

Direct retail sales; open Wed.–Sat., Apr. 1–Oct. 15, 9 A.M.–12 M., also, by appointment, "anytime I'm free."

From Rte. 20 in the village of Cazenovia (southeast of Syracuse) go 2 miles south on Rte. 13. Hidden Pond is located on a hill; a rock garden is in front of the brown-stained colonial with red doors.

"I know my plants' habits, likes, and dislikes intimately," says Nancy Hook. "When a client comes to Hidden Pond, he or she speaks only with me, not with some teenage kid who doesn't know a pansy from a peony."

Nancy Hook's business card hints at her many activities: "Perennial & Herb Plants; Fresh Cut or Dried Flowers; Flower & Herb Gardens Designed For Your Property; Garden Evaluation Consultations."

She sells plants directly from planting beds, and aside from standard perennials has many unusual border and rock garden plants, ornamental grasses, and ground covers. In the fall she has a large assortment of dried material. Each year Hook tries new plants, which she doesn't sell until they've proved to be hardy and worthwhile.

Hook is often hired by clients to view their home site and design flower beds, to suggest plants to use, and to teach clients how to care for the plants. She also gives tours a number of times each year to various groups—in the spring to view her extensive bulb plantings and in the summer to see the beds of perennials and annuals.

She adds, "Educating gardeners is very important to my business."

Stonecrop Nurseries, Inc.   PERENNIALS AND ALPINES
Rte. 301
Cold Spring, NY 10516
(Mailing address: R.R. 2, Box 371,
Cold Spring, NY 10516)
(914) 265–2000   Caroline Burgess, Manager

Direct retail sales; open Wed. and Sat. by appointment.

*Take Taconic State Pkwy. north to Rte. 301; turn left on Rte. 301;
or take Rte. 9 north to Rte. 301 (across from West Point) and turn
right; go to Dennytown Rd. and go north to Stonecrop.*

Stonecrop offers unusual perennials, annuals, half-hardy plants,
and alpines. This is how Burgess describes the nurseries:
        "Stonecrop Nurseries is modeled after an English garden
in that the visitor will be able to purchase any plant that he or
she sees in the gardens.
        "The display gardens cover some five acres and consist
of perennial borders and flower gardens, a walled garden in the
English tradition, an Alpine House and greenhouses, raised stone
beds planted with alpines, rock gardens, stream garden, cliff
garden, lagoons, and woodland gardens.
        "A visit to Stonecrop provides a good exposure to the art
of gardening, in particular the application of English gardening
principles and design to a garden in Northeastern America and
its climate."
        An interesting and attractive place to visit.

Roslyn Nursery   AZALEAS, RHODODENDRONS, RARE AND
211 Burrs La.   UNUSUAL PLANTS, TREES, EVERGREENS
Dix Hills, NY 11746
(516) 643–9347   Dr. Philip and Harriet Waldman, Owners

        Direct retail sales; open Tues.–Sat., 9 A.M.–5 P.M.; Sun., Apr.–
May, 9 A.M.–5 P.M. Also mail-order sales; catalog $2.

*Take exit 50 on Long Island Expwy.; go ¼ mile on eastbound service
road; then take a right turn onto Burrs La.; go 1 mile south to the
nursery (on right side of the street).*

Roslyn Nursery has more than 1,500 varieties of plants; this
includes rhododendrons, rhododendron species, camellias, ev-

ergreen azaleas, deciduous azaleas, *Pieris, Kalmia latifolia,* about 100 varieties of conifers, *Ilex,* evergreen shrubs such as *Cotoneaster, Daphne,* and *Pyracantha,* deciduous shrubs including *Hydrangea* and *Spiraea,* deciduous trees, ferns, ground covers, perennials, and wildflowers.

The Waldmans say the basic criteria for their plants are hardiness and beauty. Many of them, they point out, were developed by enthusiastic plant lovers who hybridize in their "backyards" for the sheer joy and hope of introducing new and superior plants.

Dr. Philip Waldman is a full-time dentist and the nursery business started as a hobby. Calling it a "hobby" now might be open to question because it has expanded to three locations with a greenhouse area totaling 40,000 square feet and 8 acres of land. The nursery propagates about 50,000 cuttings a year and also is active in hybridization, primarily with rhododendrons and azaleas.

You'll find many varieties of landscape-size plants for sale at the nursery that aren't available by mail. So if you have interests in azaleas, rhododendrons, and the like, a trip here is highly recommended.

As one visitor put it, "This is like being in a candy store."

Lyndon Lyon Greenhouses, Inc.   AFRICAN VIOLETS,
14 Mutchler St.   EXOTIC AND UNUSUAL
Dolgeville, NY 13329-1358   HOUSEPLANTS
(315) 429–8291   Paul Sorano, President

Direct retail sales; open every day, 8 A.M.–5 P.M. Also mail-order sales; catalog $1.

Located fifteen minutes off the N.Y. Thruway (Rte. 90); take exit 29-A to Rte. 169 north to Little Falls; then take Rte. 5 east to Rte. 167 north; go 6 miles to Dolgeville; on Main St., turn right on Van Buren St. and go two blocks to Mutchler St.; it's at end of the street.

Lyndon Lyon Greenhouses was founded in 1954 by Lyndon Lyon, grandfather of Paul Sorano. Sorano tells about it:

"My grandfather, Lyndon Lyon, hybridized the first 'double pink' violets in the world. He also led the way in developing the modern-day 'miniature' and 'trailing' African violets.

"We grow over two hundred and fifty varieties of African violets and over three hundred varieties of unusual houseplants, including orchids in our three greenhouses. Plants are growing on three levels which makes this the equivalent of six greenhouses.

"We're a family-owned and -operated business with all of us fully knowledgeable about the plants we grow, and we're always willing to answer questions or try to help with advice either here or on the phone.

"As our catalog only has a small sample of what we grow it's worthwhile to see us in person. We're located in a small, peaceful, and scenic village on the edge of the Adirondacks and people are welcome to just browse and/or look at our own personal collection of blooming tropical plants and such. We're here seven days a week."

If you're a gesneriad and/or tropical plant fancier—this rates three stars.

American Dahlia Society Trial Garden

Get a preview of dahlias to come. An official American Dahlia Society trial garden is located in Eisenhower Park, just in back of the Administration Building—which is just north of the intersection of Hampstead Turnpike and Newbridge Road in East Meadow, Long Island.

Trial gardens are the society's means of judging and introducing—if a flower warrants it—a new dahlia. The best viewing period is July through September.

The garden is not generally publicized because the society

has had problems with damage to the exhibits. But any person interested in dahlias is most welcome.

Henry Leuthardt Nurseries, Inc.   ESPALIERED FRUIT
Montauk Hwy.   TREES, DWARF FRUIT
East Moriches, NY 11940   TREES, BUSH FRUITS
(Mailing address: P.O. Box 666, East
Moriches, NY 11940)   Henry P. Leuthardt,
(516) 878–1387   President

Direct retail sales; open every day during digging season, Mar. 1–May 15 and Sept. 15–Dec. 15, 9 A.M.–4 P.M.; other times by appointment. Also mail-order sales; free list.

On the south shore of Long Island, 10 miles west of Westhampton; the nursery is on the north side of the Old Montauk Hwy. (County Rd. 80), halfway between Center and East Moriches.

Leuthardt sells dwarf and semidwarf fruit trees—cherry, plum, pear, peach, nectarine, apricot, and apple—the ornamental Bradford Pear, and bush fruits including currants, raspberries, gooseberries, and blueberries. He also has table and dessert grapes featuring seedless varieties that are disease resistant, will thrive in most of the eastern states, and will produce a fine wine.

But Leuthardt's forte is growing espaliered fruit trees. "Don't mean to blow my own horn," he says, "but am one of the few growers of espaliered fruit trees in the world—the only grower in the U.S. to offer the more elaborate forms of espaliers—other than simple horizontal forms."

It's the time and labor involved, he adds, that keeps most growers from trying them.

Among his more interesting forms are a six-armed Palmette Verrier Espalier, which has a shape, you might say, of a six-tined pitchfork, and the Belgian Espalier Fence, five trees planted two feet apart and trained in a diagonal lattice; the fence can be extended farther by planting more trees.

Considering what is involved in producing espaliers, Leuthardt's are reasonably priced. He has been running his espalier nursery since 1930.

If you'd like to find out more about espalier, his handbook *How to Select, Plant and Care for Dwarf Fruit Trees and Espalier Trained Fruit Trees* is available for $1. Send check or money order to the nursery.

Martin Viette Nurseries   GARDEN CENTER, NURSERY
Rte. 25-A, Northern Blvd.
East Norwich, NY 11732
(Mailing address: P.O. Box 10,
East Norwich, NY 11732)
(516) 922–5530   Russ Ireland, Owner

Direct retail sales; open every day, Mar.–Dec., 8 A.M.–6 P.M.; every day, Jan.–Feb., 9 A.M.–5 P.M.

Located on Rte. 25-A between Rte. 106 and Rte. 107; take Long Island Expwy. to exit 41-N; go north on Rte. 106 to Rte. 25-A; turn left (west) to nurseries.

Martin Viette Nurseries is a huge complex of 42 acres consisting of a complete garden center, 28,000 square feet of greenhouses, plots of perennials and bedding plants, 4 acres of nursery stock, and 16 acres devoted to growing perennials.

Sales departments consist of nursery (trees and shrubs), perennials, annuals (bedding plants), greenhouse (flowering and foliage plants), garden room (pottery, baskets, and gifts), and garden shop (tools, supplies, and garden accessories).

The nursery has a big selection of perennials, all grown

on the premises and is also known for its landscape-size specimen trees and shrubs.

Viette Nurseries has a complete horticultural library you can browse through, plantscape consultation and design planning if you'd like, and delivery and planting services if you don't want to dig in the dirt yourself..

As the holiday season approaches Viette is transformed into a Christmas wonderland where you'll find just about everything you'll need for decorations, from live, balled, plantable trees, to tree ornaments selected from around the world.

When you stop in the parking lot don't be surprised if you find yourself surrounded by Jaguars, BMWs, Cadillacs, Mercedes, and even a Rolls Royce or two. This is where residents from Long Island's "Gold Coast" shop—which means you should find first-class plant materials there.

Crosman Seed Corp.   PACKET SEEDS,
507 W. Commercial St., Crosman Terr.   GRASS SEEDS
East Rochester, NY 14445
(Mailing address: P.O. Box 110,
East Rochester, NY 14445)   William Mapstone,
(716) 586–1923   Vice President

Direct retail sales; open Mon.–Fri., 8 A.M.–5 P.M. Also mail-order sales; free seed listing.

Take Rte. 90 to Rte. 490 north to Rte. 31F, go east to Commercial St.

You might make a special trip to East Rochester to pay homage to the Crosman Seed Corp. The company, established in 1838 by C. W. Crosman, is the oldest packet seed house in the United States.

If you need a further reason for making the trip: Crosman has some 350 varieties of vegetable and flower seeds that

Vice President Mapstone says are the best customer product value in the United States. Vegetable packets start as low as 49 cents; "mammoth" 2-ounce packets of beans, peas, and corn are 59 cents; "growers" packets ranging from ¼ to 2 ounces of seeds of other vegetables sell for 89 cents; and ½-lb packets of vegetables start at $1.15. Flower seeds are 59 cents and up.

Hard to beat those prices!

George Landis Arboretum
Lape Rd., Box 186
Esperance, NY 12066
(518) 875–6935

Open every day, Mar.–Nov., daylight hours.

Take N.Y. Thruway to exit 24 (Washington Ave.); then take U.S. 20 to Esperance.

The 100 acres of the Landis Arboretum have over 2,000 varieties of conifers, magnolias, flowering cherries, flowering crab-apples, oaks, maples, beeches, lilacs, barberries, cotoneasters, viburnums, honeysuckles, azaleas, and rhododendrons.

The arboretum also has about 50 acres of nonindigenous plants from around the world, which are clearly identified. This serves as a testing ground for determining what tender trees and shrubs are suitable for northern gardens.

Other plantings include a spring bulb garden, iris and rose gardens, wildflower and fern gardens, annual and perennial gardens, a peony garden, and a quarry rock garden.

You can pick up a brochure about the arboretum at the information center, which also serves as a conference center and has over 1,000 volumes in a library and a full-time horticulturist.

Special programs are held throughout the season on such topics as pruning trees, natural history, horticulture, botany, birding, etc. You can get information about these at the center.

Legg Dahlia Gardens   DAHLIAS
1069 Hastings Rd.
Geneva, NY 14456
(315) 789–1205   Frederick Legg, Owner

Direct retail sales; open every day, July–mid-Oct., 8 A.M.–sunset. Also mail-order sales; write for list

On Rtes. 5 and 20 west of Geneva turn south at Ponderosa (traffic light), go 1½ miles (on County Rd. #6), then turn right on Hastings Rd; follow signs, 1 mile to gardens.

Legg Dahlia Gardens are a regional highlight in Geneva from August through October. No wonder—Frederick Legg who started the gardens in 1960 has more than 5,000 dahlias (over 500 different varieties) and most of them are blooming at this time. Blooms range in size from "poms," less than 2 inches across to "A," a spectacular 8 inches across. Peak bloom is about September 1.

You'll be given a clipboard when you walk through the gardens. Every dahlia variety is tagged with name and price. You can jot down your favorites so you'll know what to plant in your own garden next spring.

This is a "must" for everyone with an interest in dahlias. And if you are looking for a particular dahlia you can't find, just ask Legg. Chances are he has it somewhere.

New York State Fruit Testing   FRUIT TREES, GRAPES,
Cooperative Association   BERRIES
West North St.
Geneva, NY 14456
(Mailing address: Box 462,
Geneva, NY 14456)   David A. Gripe,
(315) 767–2205   General Manager

Direct retail sales from Mar. 15–June 1; open Mon.–Fri., year-round, 9 A.M.–4:30 P.M. Also mail-order sales; free catalog.

Located on grounds of the N.Y. State Agricultural Experiment Station in Geneva.

The New York State Fruit Testing Association (NYSFTA) was established in 1918 as a nonprofit membership association. Its purpose was to propagate new selections from the breeding program at the New York State Agricultural Experiment Station. Over the years, NYSFTA has been the first nursery to propagate some of today's most popular apples; for example, the Cortland was introduced in 1915, the Macoun in 1923, the Empire in 1966, and the Jonagold in 1968.

The catalog (it's advisable to read it in advance) describes varieties available along with helpful information, characteristics, and background. Among the many apples available are a number of "historical" apples such as the Calville Blanc, the oldest apple in the Geneva collection of more than 2,000 varieties, dating to 1598, and the Cox Orange, an important variety in England.

NYSFTA also has pears, cherries, peaches, nectarines, apricots, plums, blueberries, raspberries, blackberries, strawberries, currants, gooseberries, elderberries, grapes (including French hybrid wine grapes), and some specialty items such as mulberries, quince, currant-gooseberries, flowering cherries, and Asian pears.

Although the fruits are available for sale in Geneva only in March, April, and May, you can call the office throughout the year Monday through Friday if you have any questions.

Bayard Cutting Arboretum
Montauk Hwy.
Great River, NY
(Mailing address: P.O. Box 466,
Oakdale, NY 11769)
(516) 581–1002

Open Wed.–Sun., year-round, 10 A.M.–5 P.M.; closed Christmas Day. Walks, public buildings, and rest rooms are accessible to the handicapped. Admission fee.

On Long Island; take Heckscher State Pkwy. to Montauk Hwy. (Rte. 27A); take exit 45E to arboretum.

Using plans made by the landscape firm of Frederick Law Olmsted, William Bayard Cutting began the development of the arboretum in 1887. Several years later, with the help of Charles Sargent, then director of Boston's Arnold Arboretum, Cutting began to plant a conifer collection.

Many of these original plantings were lost during Hurricane Gloria in 1985, but the current collection of fir, spruce, pine, cypress, hemlock, yew, and other lesser-known conifers is probably still the most-extensive collection to be found on Long Island.

In addition, there are many plantings of dwarf evergreens, rhododendrons and azaleas, hollies, and oaks. Wildflowers are featured in native woodland locations, and these combined with the arboretum's ponds and streamlets attract land and aquatic birds, and occasional fox, raccoons, and other small wildlife.

With the help of a guide map you can take the Pinetum Walk, Wild Flower Walk, Rhododendron Walk, Swamp Cypress Walk, and Bird Watchers Walk.

A natural history museum with a large collection of mounted birds is in the former Cutting residence and there's also a snack bar on an enclosed porch overlooking the arboretum grounds.

Wisley Farm   DAHLIAS, FRESH CUT FLOWERS
Rte. 1, Box 556, Wayne Rd.
Hammondsport, NY 14840
(607) 569–3578   Jim Embrey, Owner

Direct retail sales; open every day, Mar. 15–Oct. 15, 9 A.M.–5 P.M. Also mail-order sales; free price list.

Take Rte. 390 to Rte. 54 north to Hammondsport; Wisley Farm is 2½ miles north of Hammondsport on Wayne Rd., at the Watkins Glen turn.

Jim and Margaret Embrey, who started their business in 1986, specialize in show-winning dahlias—which means they have some beauties. Visit their nursery when dahlias are in bloom and you're likely to see 'Alfred C,' a giant with blooms over 10 inches in diameter and which brought in 82 awards in a recent year, or 'Walter Hardisty,' whose giant white flowers raked in 166 awards that same year. Of course, there are dozens more from which to select your favorites.

Each dahlia root sold is individually wrapped and accompanied by its "pedigree" sheet; this will show you the year of its introduction, its classification according to American Dahlia Society standards, its recent record of performance at U.S. shows, and mention of any outstanding medals or certificates awarded.

"Dahlias," says Jim Embrey, "are very easy to grow, requiring no special treatment. Yet they respond remarkably to extra care, extra fertilizer, and disbudding to restrict the number of flowers to generate show-quality blooms."

Gloria Dei Nursery   MINIATURE ROSES
36 East Rd.
High Falls, NY 12440
(914) 687–9981   **Martin and Norma Kelly, Owners**

Direct retail sales; greenhouse open by appointment. Also mail-order sales; free catalog.

Nursery is 10 miles southwest of Kingston, N.Y. Directions given when making appointment.

When you buy a miniature rose from the more than 100 varieties at Gloria Dei Nursery you can be pretty sure you're getting a top-notch plant. Both Martin and Norma Kelly have been accredited judges of the American Rose Society since 1975. Their knowledge of what makes a good plant helps them carry out their goal of selling superior quality miniatures that will thrive in the garden—even for novice growers.

Martin, who has been a public-school music teacher for more than thirty years, developed an interest in growing roses in 1960. In the 1970s he and Norma became active in a local rose society that was being formed, and before long they were traveling up and down the east coast judging rose shows. Gloria Dei got its start in 1979. In 1988 both the Kellys received the Outstanding Judge Award from the New York district of the American Rose Society.

Gloria Dei's roses include many from well-known breeders and also award winners from each year.

Miniature roses, the Kellys say, can be grown with a minimum of care and in places that may be unsuitable for larger roses. These little roses are generally much hardier than their larger cousins. You can even grow them in your home on a sunny windowsill or under fluorescent lights—although they do need more light than the average houseplant.

Wood Classics, Inc.
R.D. 1, Box 455E
High Falls, NY 12440
(914) 687–7288

OUTDOOR FURNITURE

Eric and Barbara Goodwin,
Owners

Garden showroom open Mon.–Fri., 9:30 A.M.–4:30 P.M., Sat., 9:30 A.M.–1 P.M. Also mail-order sales; catalog $2.

About two hours north of New York City, between Rte. 209 and N.Y. Thruway. Call for directions from High Falls because the company is way back in the woods and hard to find.

Wood Classics manufactures classic British and American styles of furniture using only two woods, teak and mahogany. The company feels these are the best woods for outdoor furniture because neither needs any protection from the weather and both can be stored outside year-round. The woods won't rot, split, or splinter, and they weather to an even silvery gray.

The small staff of the family-owned business handcrafts all the furniture, right down to the wooden pegs, in High Falls. Furniture is made with true mortise and tenon joinery wherever appropriate. There is no exposed metal to rust or stain.

You can choose the furniture in an easy-to-assemble kit form or completely assembled and delivered to your home anywhere in the Northeast.

In the showroom, samples of the Wood Classics furniture are displayed, along with similar items from competitors. Some dimensions of Wood Classics furniture are scaled to fit those Americans usually prefer rather than what is the norm in Europe. Therefore, visitors have a chance to examine all styles and come to their own conclusions regarding comfort as well as beauty and durability.

The Goodwins say their products are usually the winners.

Bonsai East, Inc,   BONSAI
273 Main St., 2nd floor
Huntington, NY 11743   Peter Bringer, President
(516) 271–3278   Rose Bringer, Secretary

Direct retail sales; hours vary by season; call ahead. Greenhouse open by appointment only.

Take Rte. 110 N to 25A (Main St.) in Huntington; turn left one-half block west of Rte. 110; it is on the north side of the street, on the second floor—above a card shop.

Bonsai East has a good variety of indoor and outdoor bonsai, both imported and domestic, with plants starting at a reasonable $25. And if you want to create your own bonsai, you'll find a large selection of pre-bonsai plants, plus containers, stands, tools, wire, soil, and books. Members of the Bonsai Society get a 15 percent discount.

Bonsai East reminds customers that the company is there not just to sell bonsai, but also to answer any and all questions they may have, including bonsai first-aid advice. And people who are going on vacation can use the bonsai sitting services.

Several bonsai experts give classes on creating bonsai throughout the year; for more information call or write.

Panfield Nurseries   NURSERY, LANDSCAPING SERVICES
322 Southdown Rd.
Huntington, NY 11743
(516) 427–0112   **Thomas Paterson, President**

Direct retail sales; nursery and garden center open Mon.–Sat., Apr.–June and Sept.–Nov., 9 A.M. to 5 P.M.; Mon.–Fri. only, July–Aug., closed Dec.–Mar.

Take Rte. 110 to Huntington, then go north to Southdown Rd.; the nursery is at the end of the road in Lloyd Harbor.

Panfield Nurseries emphasizes woodland perennials, ferns, and meadow flowers and also has trees (including some unusual, large specimens for landscape use), shrubs, and ground covers. To give customers a better idea of garden possibilities they can browse through a perennial garden, a woodland garden, a gazebo garden, and a Japanese garden.

Paterson, whose father started the nursery in 1931, says, "Our landscape department specializes in naturalistic plantings featuring low-maintenance native plants and plants that attract birds and wildlife. We prefer dry stone walls to railroad ties."

The nursery staff is experienced in installing small pond gardens and rock gardens as well as the gardens on display. The nursery also does landscape-construction projects such as decks, patios, and fences.

Smirnow's Sons   TREE PEONIES
11 Oakwood Dr. W.
Huntington, NY 11743
(516) 421–0836   Robert Smirnow, Owner

Mail-order sales only; catalog $2.

Smirnow's Sons, founded by Louis Smirnow in 1940, is one of the oldest tree peony businesses in the country. The company specializes in Japanese tree peonies, but other types are available on request; the Smirnows have a worldwide network for obtaining very rare plants. Louis Smirnow introduced Chinese tree peonies to the United States when China first "opened up" in the late 1970s and early 1980s; these can be obtained in quantity by special order.

Tree peonies are more like shrubs with woody stems than trees. They're easy to grow, but growth is slow, which is why they can be expensive. Their beauty is in their massive flowers, some more than 10 inches, with petals that have the texture of crepe paper, ruffled or crinkled. Of all the types, the Japanese are often considered the most beautiful with their narrow foliage and broad flower petals.

Louis Smirnow had good reason to say that a tree peony is the "king of the garden."

Cornell Plantations

The Arboretum, Botanical Garden, and Natural Areas of Cornell
University
One Plantation Rd.
Ithaca, NY 14850-2799
(607) 255-3020

Open every day, sunrise to sunset; Garden gift shop open Mon.–
Fri., year-round, 8 A.M.–4 P.M.; Sat.–Sun., mid-Apr.–Dec., 11 A.M.–5
P.M.

*From Rte. 13 in Ithaca, take Rte. 79 east for 1²/₁₀ miles; then bear left
onto Rte. 366; go 1¹/₁₀ miles, then turn left onto Judd Falls Rd.; take
the first right after stop sign (⁴/₁₀ mile) and follow the signs.*

Cornell Plantations includes 3,000 acres so the best way to start
a tour, if you're not familiar with the area, is to stop at the
headquarters, which includes offices and the garden gift shop.
Here you can pick up a map, which you can use for a driving
tour of the arboretum as well as stops at various gardens and
areas that interest you most.

Among the places to visit in the botanical garden are the
rock garden, peony garden, herb garden, heritage garden, and
the international crop and weed garden. The arboretum includes areas of flowering trees, nut trees, magnolias, water lilies
and aquatic plants, a sculpture garden, conifers, lilacs, and various overlooks. Special guided tours can be arranged by making
advance reservations.

The plantations offer a continuing education program,
with courses such as "Growing Gourmet Vegetables," "Flowering Shrubs," the "Making of a Fragrant Garden," and "Ikebana," the Japanese art of flower arrangement. Some are
single-session classes, held on Saturdays, which make them fea-
sible for interested people who live at some distance from Ithaca.

For information about these and other activities write or

call the plantations' office. By becoming a "participant" of Cornell Plantations, for $6 per year (tax deductible), you will receive quarterly bulletins plus other regular mailings.

Hollowbrook Pottery and Tile   GARDEN CERAMICS
Box 413, Hollowbrook Rd.
(Studio on Anton Pl.)
Lake Peekskill, NY 10537   Roger L. Baumann,
(914) 526–3786   Owner

Direct retail sales; studio showroom open Tues.–Sun., year-round, 9 A.M.–5 P.M.; suggest a phone call first. Also mail-order sales; free color catalog with retail and wholesale price list.

Located in Westchester County, one hour north of Manhattan; take Taconic Pkwy. to Rte. 6; go left on 6W for 1³⁄₁₀ miles to Mill Rd.; turn right on Mill Rd. and travel for 1⁷⁄₁₀ miles to light; go left on Peekskill Hollow Rd. for 2⁴⁄₁₀ miles to next light (town of Putnam Valley); go straight; the first road on the left is Anton Pl.; the studio is the last place on left.

Handmade stoneware tile, for poolside, spa, patio, and garden paths, and stoneware planters are part of the line of ceramics crafted by Roger Baumann. Potential buyers have a chance to look over these items as well as many others in the studio showroom, nursery, greenhouse, and galleries.

Baumann started Hollowbrook Pottery and Tile in 1976 and he says, "We have always used the finest stoneware clays (we blend and make our own as we do the glazes we use). Stoneware is extremely durable and our planters withstand the harshest of winters; so it is much easier for the gardener to winter over large plants without bringing them inside.

"We offer a full design service to help our clients create the look or environment that they want. Our commitment to function and quality plus our willingness to work hand in hand with the customer has always been foremost in our business."

Seagulls Landing Orchids   ORCHIDS
1702 Rte. 25-A
Laurel Hollow, NY 11791
(Mailing address: P.O. Box 388
Glen Head, Long Island, NY
11545)
(516) 367–6336   Shell Kanzer, Owner

Direct retail sales; open Tues.–Sat., 10 A.M.–5 P.M., Sun., 11
A.M.–5 P.M.; closed Monday. Also mail-order sales; free catalog.

*On the north shore of Long Island on Route 25-A, 3 miles east of Rte.
106 and 1½ miles west of Cold Spring Harbor.*

In 1972 (the year Kanzer founded his company) the word *mini-cat* was born—a combination of the words *miniature* and *cattleya* that Kanzer used to describe the miniature cattleyas he was hybridizing. Today he's the largest grower of these in the world. In fact, mini-cat is now a generic word used throughout orchiddom.

In addition to the mini-cats, Seagulls Landing sells large plants of cattleyas, phalaenopses, dendrobiums, and vandas, along with orchid-growing supplies.

Kanzer exports to more than a dozen countries and says each year the nursery is visited by growers from all over the world.

"We specialize in orchids that can be grown in the home as houseplants," he adds. "We teach visitors how to grow and we're always available for advice."

Kimberly Garden   PERENNIALS
R.R. 1, Box 44G Oregon Hill Rd.
Lisle, NY 13797   David and Kimberly
(607) 849–6554   Armstrong, Owners

Mail-order sales only; catalog $2 (deductible).

Perennial Passion, the catalog of Kimberly Garden, is a beautiful presentation on glossy paper with many sketches of perennials and much information—about perennials, the Armstrongs, Kimberly Garden, etc.

David Armstrong is not only a horticulturist, as you'll soon discover after sending for the catalog. He also writes and sends letters (three-page letters filled with information such as that listed above) to his customers and potential customers twice a year. You'll definitely get your two dollars' worth.

Both Armstrongs had horticultural educations, and what they also have is enthusiasm—especially about gardening and perennials. They offer more than fifty varieties, shipped in containers they call "Kimtainers"—fresh and vigorous and ready to grow.

Recommended: Send for the catalog.

Florentine Craftsmen, Inc.   GARDEN ORNAMENTS
46–24 28th St.
Long Island City, NY 11101
(212) 532–3926   Graham G. Brown,
(718) 937–7632   President

Direct retail sales; showroom open Mon.–Fri., 8:30 A.M.–4:30 P.M. Also mail-order sales; catalog $4.

In Long Island City, three minutes from Queensboro Bridge or Queens Midtown Tunnel.

Since 1923 Florentine Craftsmen has been selling domestic and imported garden ornaments such as fountains, vases and urns, statuary, birdbaths, sundials, and cast-aluminum furniture.

Before visiting their showroom it might be a good idea to orient yourself by ordering a copy of the catalog and studying it first. In its fifty-six pages dozens of items are illustrated.

A few examples are a sailboat weather vane of hand-hammered copper (also available in 24-karat gold leaf), a curved cast-stone bench, St. Francis in numerous versions in lead, a cupid supporting a sundial, a ram's head wall mask, a lead figure of a kneeling girl holding a lotus blossom, a cast-iron whippet—life-size, and a Peter Pan fountain with recirculating pump, 8 feet, 8 inches high, which sells for $12,950 FOB in Long Island City.

But the company's particular niche in the industry, says Graham Brown, is its ability to custom make designs and sizes of heavy cast-aluminum furniture. Several pages of furniture are shown in the catalog—chairs, benches, glass-topped tables of various sizes, and a chaise lounge. Prices run from about $575 for a side chair to $2,750 for the chaise.

The furniture should last several lifetimes.

John Scheepers, Inc.   FLOWERING BULBS, PERENNIALS
R.D. 6, Phillipsburg Rd.
Middletown, NY 10940
(914) 342–1135   Steven van Eeden, Manager

Mail-order sales only; two full-color catalogs (spring and fall) plus seasonal brochures $3.

After being a Wall Street institution for more than seventy-five years, John Scheepers, Inc. moved out to Middletown. Founded in 1905 by John Scheepers, the company emphasizes that all of its plant material is of the highest quality. Most of this is grown on Scheepers's farm in Holland with perennials being grown in the United States. Bulbs range from *Alstroemeria* to *Zephyranthes*—with everything in between.

If you have never seen Scheepers's catalogs, by all means, send in your $3. They're well worth it. And if you are familiar with the catalogs, you're probably getting them regularly.

⚘ Innisfree Garden

Tyrrel Rd.
Millbrook, NY 12545
(914) 677–8000

Open Wed.–Fri., May–Oct., 10 A.M.–4 P.M., Sat.–Sun., 11 A.M.–
5 P.M.; closed Mon.–Tues., except for Mon. legal holidays. Admission
fee charged on Sat. and Sun.; other days admission free.

*Take Taconic Pkwy. to Rte. 44; the garden is 1 mile from Rte. 44 on
Tyrrel Rd.*

Innisfree Garden is a unique garden designed by Walter Beck,
a student of Oriental art. He began building the garden in 1930
and continued for twenty-two years.

The basic design is what is sometimes known in the Orient as a "cup garden." Beginning with a lake, which is the low-
est floor of the garden, Beck brought the surroundings under
control, using streams and waterfalls, terraces, retaining walls,
and rocks along with plantings. Everything was designed to keep
specific areas "in tension or in motion" so that each would be a
garden picture.

⚘ Mary Flagler Cary Arboretum

Rte. 44A
Millbrook, NY 12545
(Mailing address: Institute of Ecosystem Studies, Box AB, Millbrook, NY 12545)
(914) 677–5358

Open Mon.–Sat., May 1–Sept. 30, 9 A.M.–6 P.M., Sun., 1 P.M.–6
P.M.; Mon.–Sat., Oct. 1–Apr. 30, 9 A.M.–4 P.M., Sun., 1 P.M.–4 P.M.;
closed for major holidays. Trails and internal roads closed during deer-
hunting season and inclement weather.

Take Taconic Pkwy. to Rte. 44; go east 2 miles to Rte. 44A; turn left;
the arboretum's Gifford House Visitor and Education Center is 1 mile
on the left.

The Mary Flagler Cary Arboretum is the base for the New York
Botanical Garden's Institute of Ecosystem Studies. An "ecosystem" could be called the complex of a living community—plants,
animals, microbes—and its physical environment, functioning
together as an ecological unit. Disturbances in an ecosystem may
be of human origin, as in the clear-cutting of a forest or the
effects of air pollution, or of natural origin, such as a lightning
strike or flood.

Specific research areas at the Cary Arboretum include
landscape ecology, plant-animal interaction, chemical ecology,
and wildlife management. Its purpose is to improve predictions
about the consequence of human interactions with the environment and so provide better information for formulating important public policy.

In the arboretum you'll have a chance to observe local
ecology and ecologically sound landscaping techniques. Among
the areas you might find interesting are the Fern Glen where
native North American ferns as well as ferns from Europe and
Asia are tested for their hardiness in this climate; the Meadow
Garden, which is a demonstration of a landscape that is beautiful year-round but requires minimal labor and energy to
maintain; and the Perennial Garden, which shows how effective
the use of low-maintenance perennials can be.

On the first and third Sundays of each month you can
attend a free ecology program designed to interest nature lovers of all ages.

Stop at the Gifford House Visitor and Education Center
for information about the arboretum and its programs.

The Conservatory Garden, Central Park
Fifth Ave. at 105th St.
New York, NY 10128
(212) 397–3150

Open every day, 8 A.M.–dusk.

In the 6 acres of the Conservatory Garden you'll find formal plantings of crabapple trees, evergreens, 20,000 tulips in the spring and 5,000 chrysanthemums in the fall, flowering Japanese quince, white-flowering spirea, lilac trees, some 3,500 perennials, wildflowers, ferns, wisteria, roses, and more.

The Conservatory Garden is separated from the rest of the park with a wrought-iron fence and three gates. The main gate, on Fifth Avenue, is the ornate Vanderbilt Gate, which was made in Paris in 1894 for the Vanderbilt mansion at Fifty-eighth Street and Fifth Avenue. After the mansion was demolished the gate was given to the city.

The reason that the garden is called the Conservatory Garden is because it's on the former site of a complex of conservatories that were built in 1899 but were removed in 1934 because of the rising costs of maintaining them.

For a map and guide to the garden call the Central Park Information Center at (212) 397–3156, or write to the Central Park Conservancy, 830 Fifth Ave., New York, NY 10021.

The Father of American Landscape Architecture

Frederick Law Olmsted (1822–1903) designed so many outstanding parks, gardens, and estates in the latter half of the nineteenth century that at times you have to look hard to find anything from that era that hadn't been on his drawing board.

Olmsted served as an apprentice topographic engineer for a brief period, then attended lectures in science and engineering at Yale, became interested in scientific farming, and during a long stay in Europe observed English landscaping.

When Central Park in New York City was proposed in 1857, a plan developed by Olmsted along with Calvert Vaux, a young British architect, won first prize in the competition with thirty other entrants.

This was one of the first times in the United States that art was applied to nature in the form of a public park. The publicity Olmsted got from this kept him busy for most of the rest of his life.

Among his works are Fairmont Park in Philadelphia; Belle Island Park in Detroit; the grounds surrounding the Capitol in Washington, D.C.; the site for the Chicago World's Columbian Exposition, which was later redesigned as Jackson Park; the campuses of Stanford University and Smith College; the Biltmore Estate in Asheville, North Carolina; the Arnold Arboretum in Boston; the Highland Botanical Park in Rochester, New York; the Bayard Cutting Arboretum on Long Island; and the formal gardens of the Auchincloss estate, Hammersmith Farm in Newport (where the wedding reception of Jacqueline Bouvier and John F. Kennedy was held).

Many think he also designed Boston's Public Garden, but that was first planned in 1838 and redesigned in 1852. However, he did design an extensive system of parkways and parks for Boston and neighboring Brookline, Massachusetts.

Rainbow Violets   AFRICAN VIOLETS
1609 Michigan Ave.
Niagara Falls, NY 14305   Richard M. Wasmund,
(716) 282–8936 (after 6 P.M.)   Owner

Direct retail sales, Sat. and Sun., by appointment (Wasmund will give you directions when you call). Also mail-order sales; free list.

Wasmund has been hybridizing violets since the early 1970s and sells, primarily, his own hybrids. But he usually has the new varieties from Granger Gardens and Lyndon Lyons on hand. Currently he has over sixty rainbow varieties for sale—including standards, miniatures, and semiminiatures.

Wasmund doesn't advertise in garden magazines because he sells through several dozen distributors. But he says, "Although I'm a commercial member of many clubs, I'm not really in it for the money. I enjoy hybridizing and giving people a good show plant and a beautiful blossom."

S. Scherer & Sons   AQUATIC PLANTS, GARDEN POOLS
104 Waterside Rd.
Northport, NY 11768
(516) 261–7432   Robert W. Scherer, Owner

Direct retail sales; open Mon.–Sat., 8 A.M.–5:30 P.M., Sun., 9 A.M.–4 P.M. Also mail-order sales; free brochure.

Take exit 53N on the Long Island Expwy. or exit SM-1 north on the Northern State Pkwy.; go north on Sunken Meadow Pkwy. to exit SM-5; go west on Rte. 25A about 4 miles; turn right at Jimmy Jay's Restaurant (Waterside Rd.); Scherer's is ¾ mile north on the right.

Scherer's grows and sells tropical and hardy water plants—water lilies—day- and night-blooming plants, shallow water and bog plants, floating plants, water lotus, oxygenating plants, and dwarf rock garden plants. The company is one of the largest growers of aquatic plants in the United States and the largest in New York State.

You can also buy cut water lily flowers ready to be placed in your pool; they're a great decorating idea for special occasions, weddings, or garden parties, or whenever you want an immediate effect.

Scherer's also sells fiberglass pools, pool heaters, pumps, waterfalls—everything needed for a garden pool (even goldfish, Japanese Koi, and catfish).

The company goes back three generations. It was founded by Sigmund Scherer, who was born in Switzerland and got horticulture training there while an apprentice at the Royal Gardens. Today his grandson Robert is the owner and great-grandson Robert Walton Thomas Scherer has recently joined the firm.

One thing the company insists on is that salespeople give each customer full personal attention, whether buying one item or buying an entire pool setup. In fact, if you're buying the latter, the salesperson will explain every procedure in detail—even if it takes several hours. So if you have any questions, you can count on getting thorough and detailed answers.

John H. Gordon Jr., Grower   NUT AND CROPPING
1385 Campbell Blvd.   TREES, P.Y.O. NUTS
North Tonawanda, NY 14120
(716) 691–9371   John H. Gordon, Jr., Owner

Direct retail sales; call first (best time is before 8 A.M. and evenings). Also mail-order sales; free list.

North Tonawanda is between Buffalo and Niagara Falls; on N.Y. Rte. 270, 4 miles north of N.Y. Rte. 263.

Among the tree varieties available from Gordon are almonds, filbert, tree hazel, sweet chestnut, shagbark and shellbark hickories, northern pecan, heartnut, and black walnut. Most can be purchased as seedlings or as seeds. Gordon has extensive information about growing nut trees, and much information is in pamphlet form.

An advantage of visiting the farm is that you can see the trees fruiting, save shipping charges, and find many specials that are not listed. Also, you can pick your own (P.Y.O.) nuts or buy already picked samples.

Most important, you can get advice and growing suggestions from Gordon, who has been operating his farm since 1975 and has had extensive experience with cropping trees.

Old Westbury Gardens
71 Old Westbury Rd.
Old Westbury, NY 11568
(Mailing address: P.O. Box 430, Old Westbury, NY 11568)
(516) 333–0048; (516) 333–0175

Open Wed.–Sun. and all holidays, last Sat. in Apr. through first
Sun. in Nov., 10 A.M.–5 P.M. Admission fee charged for gardens with
additional charge for Westbury House.

*Take Long Island Expwy. to exit 39S; continue on eastbound service
road to Old Westbury Rd. and turn right; the entrance is less than 1
mile ahead, on the left side.*

Old Westbury Gardens was built in the early twentieth century
to recreate an English country estate. The John S. Phipps family lived in it to the 1950s, and in 1959 the 100-acre estate was
incorporated as a nonprofit institution for the enjoyment of the
public.

The house, which is an optional tour, is in the style of a
Charles II manor house and is furnished with English antiques.
Fresh flowers in almost every room add to the sense that a fam-
ily is still living there.

The gardens were designed by the same architect who
designed the house. Among the highlights are the Boxwood
Garden, which was planted with giant boxwood that was already over 100 years old when it was brought from Virginia;
the Cottage Garden, where a little child's thatched cottage is
surrounded by a miniature garden; and the Walled Garden, with
over 2 acres of herbaceous borders, ornamental pools and
fountains, and changing floral displays beginning with tulips in
May and progressing to masses of chrysanthemums in October.
In early summer there are delphiniums, roses, canterbury bells,
iris, and many other labeled perennials and annuals. The selection of plants, which are compatible in color, height, texture,

and season of bloom, offers a variety of ideas for visitors to use in their own gardens.

There are also several small demonstration gardens that provide visitors with ideas and designs that can be easily incorporated into their own gardens. Among these are an All-America Rose Selections test garden, an herb garden, and a Japanese-style garden.

Numerous workshops and other educational programs are offered throughout the year, with a special emphasis on children's programs. For information about these call or write the garden.

✿ Planting Fields Arboretum

Planting Fields Rd.
Oyster Bay, NY 11771
(516) 922–9201

Open every day, year-round, 9 A.M.–5 P.M.; closed Christmas Day. Admission fee charged.

Take the Long Island Expwy. to exit 29 north (Glen Cove Rd.), go north to Rte. 25A (Northern Blvd.); turn right (east) onto Rte. 25A; go past C. W. Post College and Rte. 107, then turn left (north) onto Wolver Hollow Rd.; at the end, turn right onto Chicken Valley Rd.; turn right onto Planting Fields Rd.; the entrance is about 1 mile on the right.

With more than 400 acres of gardens, lawns, and natural woodlands, Planting Fields is a world-famous showplace.

Two greenhouse complexes total over 1½ acres. The Camellia Greenhouse displays the oldest and largest camellia collection under glass and is at its height during January, February, and March. You'll also see bougainvillea and allamanda collections plus bromeliads, cactus and succulents, orchids, begonias, and ferns. The main conservatory features seasonal displays.

Nearly 1,000 different species are planted in the two Rhododendron Parks and the Azalea Walk. Bloom begins in early April and continues through June. You'll also see hundreds of specimen trees, both imported and native, gracing the lawns and driveways.

And you'll learn your ABCs in the Synoptic Garden. It's a 5-acre alphabetical planting (by botanical name) of ornamental trees and shrubs desirable for the Long Island area, starting with *Abelia* and ending with *Zenobia*.

At the Arboretum Center a herbarium of over 10,000 pressed specimens is available for study and identification, and you'll find a wide selection of books in the Horticultural Library. A number of noncredit, horticulturally related courses are offered throughout the year.

One of the highlights of the year is the annual fall flower and landscape show. For specific dates and information about available courses call or write Planting Fields.

Stiles Gardens   GLADIOLUS BLOOMS AND BULBS
1798 Stiles Rd., R.F.D. 1
Penn Yan, NY 14527–9640
(315) 536–6881   Leon Stiles, Hobbyist

Direct retail sales, open "whenever the customer can find me home" (call ahead to make sure). Also mail-order sales; free list.

On Stiles Rd., ½ mile east of Penn Yan, just south of Rte. 54.

Leon Stiles and his wife, Eleanor, started Stiles Gardens as a retirement hobby in 1984. Stiles handles his own introductions and one of his most popular is his Silver Ripples—silver-white blooms with a faint pink—which is often used by florists for

wedding arrangements. Stiles also has a number of glads from
other hybridizers.

The prices here are very reasonable and include bargain
assortments of many varieties that have been carried on test.

Stiles's gardens are open to visitors all summer (please,
adults only) and he'll be happy to discuss glads with you. And
if you're a hybridizer and have something you believe worthy
of introduction, he'd like to include a sample in his trial gardens.

Stonehurst Rare Plants   RARE AND DWARF PLANTS,
1 Stonehurst Ct.   JAPANESE MAPLES
Pomona, NY 10970   Howard Kellerman, M.D.,
(914) 354—4049; (914) 354—0052   Owner

Direct retail sales; call or write ahead. Also mail-order sales;
catalog $1.

*Take exit 14 (Spring Valley) on N.Y. Thruway; Pomona is approxi-
mately 5 miles north; call for directions in Pomona.*

Stonehurst Rare Plants is for connoisseurs. If you're interested
in dwarf and unusual conifers, Japanese maples, rare dwarf
rhododendrons, and companion plants, this is an absolute must.

This is *not* a commercial nursery. "Sale of these plants,"
says Kellerman, "is secondary to our main interest in collecting
and studying the dwarf conifers. Surplus plants became available and it was decided to make these available to other serious
collectors."

Although Kellerman will ship plants, he strongly advises
a personal visit and inspections. Written descriptions of rare plant
material are poor substitutes for seeing the actual plant, he says.
Also, his inventory changes constantly, much faster than printed
lists can be updated. Because most of the plants are grown in

containers, they can be taken from the nursery at any time of year; shipping, however, is limited to April, May, September, and October.

Here's an example of what you will find there: There are well over 200 choicest cultivars of Japanese maples with 39 listings under *Acer palmatum dissectum* alone.

St. Lawrence Nurseries

R.D. 2
Potsdam, NY 13676
(315) 265–6739

FRUIT AND NUT TREES

Bill and Diana MacKentley,
Owners

Direct retail sales; open Mon.–Sat., Apr.–mid-May and Nov., daytime; visitors welcome other times, but call first. Also mail-order sales; free catalog.

From Potsdam take Rte. 345 north toward Madrid. Nurseries are at top of the fourth hill out, on the left.

The MacKentleys produce hardy, northern-grown (Zones 3 and 4) fruit and nut trees and bush fruits—with the emphasis on *hardy*.

"Gardeners who have had many failures due to winter damage," says Diana MacKentley, "should try us. We guarantee the survival of our trees if cared for adequately and will replace any tree that dies or doesn't leaf out in the first season."

The nursery was started in the 1920s by Fred Ashworth, a northern New York plant breeder who was cofounder of North American Fruit Explorers (NAFEX). Bill MacKentley, who served as Ashworth's apprentice, decided to carry on the work and bought the nursery after Ashworth's death.

St. Lawrence has pears, cherries, plums, grapes, blueberries, currants, lingonberries, black walnuts, butternuts, and various yard trees. The nursery also has 110 varieties of apples, most of them heirloom apples with such names as Alexander and Antonovka (of Russian parentage), the Royalty Crab (from Saskatoon), the Prairie Spy, the Jordan Russet, and the Leafland Greening (all of unknown parentage).

When you visit the nursery you won't find a number of well-known apples—red and yellow delicious, Baldwin, Jonathan, and Rome Beauty. The reason is that these trees just can't stand the region's most devastating winters. They might last a series of mild winters, only to be "zapped" when a test winter comes along.

A "test winter," according to the MacKentleys, which comes along every ten years or so, is one where temperature plunges to −50°F.

Unless you live near the Arctic Circle, these trees should do well for you.

Trees are dug only in April to May or early November, but visitors are welcome at the nursery at any time. Best to call ahead, however, to make sure someone will be there.

🦎 Highland Botanical Park

180 Reservoir Ave.
Rochester, NY 14620
(716) 244–8079

Aboretum open daily, dawn to dusk; conservatory open Tues.–Sun., 10 A.M.–6 P.M.; Wed., 10 A.M.–8 P.M.; closed Mon. and Christmas Day.

From I-490, exit at S. Goodman St.; go south to park; from I-390 exit at E. Henrietta Rd.; go north to park.

Highland Park, which covers more than 150 acres, is one of the oldest public arboretums or "tree gardens" in the country. Frederick Law Olmsted designed it and the park opened in 1888.

The Lamberton Conservatory is at the corner of Reservoir Drive and South Avenue. Here you can pick up a guide and map to the park, including a self-guided walking tour. Highland Park's collections range from azaleas to yews with a woodland garden, a horse-chestnut collection, Japanese maple collection, magnolia collection, pinetum, pansy bed, rock garden, and its highlight—the Lilac Collection.

The Lilac Collection covers 22 acres and each May the week-long Lilac Festival draws visitors from around the world—with good reason. The Highland Park Lilac Collection is the largest in the world, representing more than 500 varieties that have been collected since 1905. A deep sky-blue 'President Lincoln,' introduced in 1916, is still considered to be one of the best of the blue lilacs. 'Rochester,' a creamy white variety introduced in 1963, commemorates the city that has become synonymous with lilacs.

The Lamberton Conservatory has numerous collections of plants not hardy in the Rochester climate, with a tropical forest display and collections of exotic plants, desert plants, house plants, and seasonal floral displays, which are changed five times a year. Near the conservatory is the Garden Center of Rochester with a 3,000-volume library and various display gardens, old-fashioned rose bed, fern bed, and a thirteenth-century herb garden.

For the exact date of the annual lilac festival, which lasts for ten days in May, call or write the park.

Saxton Gardens   DAYLILIES
1 First St.
Saratoga Springs, NY 12866   Stanley E. Saxton,
(518) 584–4697   Owner

Direct retail sales; call for appointment. Also mail-order sales; catalog 40 cents.

On Rte. 87 take exit 15; go three stoplights to East Ave., turn right and go to the end of the street; turn left, Saxton Gardens is two blocks ahead on the corner.

Stanley Saxton has been breeding daylilies since the 1940s and was a charter member of the American Hemerocallis Society. About his plants he says, "In our cold mountain garden it is essential that they be extremely hardy and strong growers. All the plants we offer grow well under these adverse conditions."

For especially rugged conditions Saxton recommends his "Adirondack Strain," which he says is selected for beautiful flowers, many buds, and long season of bloom.

His plants are reasonably priced, especially his tetraploids for landscaping. These come from the thousands of tet seedlings that he grows and, he says, they are as beautiful as the best of new daylilies. However, they are not different enough from other named varieties, so they remain nameless. For anyone who needs a quantity of plants, this is a best buy.

Saxton recommends a book for all daylily growers, the *Daylily Encyclopedia*. With 176 pages and handy pocket size, it has information about the basic forms of daylily bloom, chapters on culture, bloom sequence, and award-winning cultivars as well as specific details about 1,000 daylilies. Price when ordered from Saxton Gardens is $13.75, postpaid.

Sprainbrook Nursery, Inc.   NURSERY, GARDEN CENTER
448 Underhill Rd.
Scarsdale, NY 10530
(914) 723–2382   **Alfred H. Krautter, President**

Direct retail sales; open Mon.–Sat., 8 A.M.–5:30 P.M., Sun., 9 A.M.–4:30 P.M.

Take exit 7 on N.Y. Thruway (Rte. 87); go right on Ashford Ave., then turn left onto Sprain Rd. just after Ardsley Middle School; follow Sprain Rd. to Underhill Rd. and nursery.

Trees, shrubs, hundreds of varieties of perennials, tropical plants, annuals—you can shop for a huge selection of these and more at Sprainbrook Nursery. Since its founding in 1944, the strength of Sprainbrook, says Krautter, has always been to propagate, grow, and produce its own plants. Many perennials are wintered over in unheated outdoor frames to make sure they can withstand the rigors of Westchester winters.

When you get to Sprainbrook you can get a catalog, which also provides cultural information. And be sure to pick up a copy of the nursery map. You'll need it. The nursery includes nineteen greenhouses, special sales areas for perennials, roses, mums, dogwoods, evergreens, magnolias, containerized nursery stock, a fertilizer shed, a perennial display garden, a woodland plants display garden, a pool, and a garden center and office.

The first weekend in March is the annual "Spring Weekend" when everything at the nursery is on sale and when you can ask questions of the staff, talk to factory representatives from many manufacturers of garden equipment and supplies, and when you can get free consultations on landscape design.

Floyd Cove Nursery   DAYLILIES
11 Shipyard La.
Setauket, NY 11733–3038
(516) 751–1806   Patrick M. Stamile, President

Direct retail sales; open every day, July–Aug., 10 A.M.–4 P.M. Also mail-order sales; catalog $1 (deductible).

Take Long Island Expwy. (Rte. 495) east to exit 62; go north on Nicolls Rd. (Rte. 97) to the end; then go right on Rte. 25-A east for 1½ miles; turn left onto Main St.; the nursery is 1,000 feet north on the right.

Begun in 1981 by Stamile, the nursery has become well known for its hundreds of varieties of hemerocallis, featuring some of the newest and finest available, including many Stamile hybrids.

This is a good place to become acquainted with daylilies during their peak bloom period—usually July and August.

Of special interest to daylily fanciers: The nursery is also the site of a national display garden of the American Hemerocallis Society.

From Taters to *Vitis vinifera*

In the past ten years some major changes have taken place on Long Island. Potato fields are being replaced by vineyards. Growers are proving that the finest wine grapes aren't limited to California or France. In fact, there are few regions throughout the world that offer the climate, soil characteristics, and unique growing conditions so essential to the production of premium wines like that of eastern Long Island.

There are many vineyards throughout the area that offer regular tours (and wine tastings). If you're interested in the culture of classic *vinefera* varieties, such as Chardonnay, Pinot Noir, Cabernet Sauvignon, Merlot, and Riesling, you might contact some of the following vineyards.

> Hargrave Vineyard, Route 48, Cutchogue, NY 11935; (516) 734–5158
>
> Jamesport Vineyards, Inc., Route 25, Jamesport, NY 11947; (516) 364–3633
>
> Peconic Bay Vineyards, Route 25, Cutchogue, NY 11935; (516) 734–7361
>
> Pindar Vineyards, Route 25, Peconic, NY 11958; (516) 734–6200

For more information and a brochure call the Long Island Grape Growers Association, Inc., (516) 727–6464.

To get a brochure listing vineyards in the Lake Erie District, the Finger Lakes District, and the Hudson River Region, call or write the New York Wine and Grape Foundation, Liberty Street, Penn Yan, NY 14527; (315) 536–7442.

Carlson's Gardens   AZALEAS, RHODODENDRONS,
Box 305   MOUNTAIN LAURELS, DOGWOODS,
South Salem, NY 10590   LILACS
(914) 763–5958   Bob and Jan Carlson, Owners

Direct retail sales by appointment; open spring, summer, and fall; usually available every day during daylight hours. Also mail-order sales; catalogs (two years) $2 (deductible).

Located 50 miles north of New York City. Detailed directions given at the time the appointment is made.

The Carlsons, who've been in business since 1968, say theirs is the largest selection of "northern grown and acclimated" azaleas and rhododendrons grown in the U.S. Department of Agriculture's Zone 6A ($-10°$F) *without* winter protection. They emphasize these are not grown under glass or plastic. Sizes sold are large enough to be "landscapable," and also large and hardy enough to survive and thrive when planted directly in customers' gardens.

In addition to their more than thirty-five years of growing experience, they have a large computer data base of records to keep tabs on the more than 1,500 varieties. Included among these are native azaleas, a number of which are endangered species. These have *not* been collected from the wild but are nursery grown from cuttings or from seeds obtained from the Carlsons' stock plants and those of azalea specialists around the country.

Among their deciduous and evergreen azaleas are varieties of Knaphill-Exbury, Robin Hill, North Tisbury, Gable, Great Lakes, Glenn Dale, and Petite. Rhododendrons include Yakusimanum, Dexter, and Shammarello. You'll also find a selection of mountain laurels and lilacs.

The Carlsons are happy to give advice and suggestions to each individual who is interested in these beautiful plants.

Just give them a call—early morning or early evening is the best
time to catch them away from the gardens. Ask for Jan or Bob
because

> You love azaleas, both early and late—
> You never bother with colors you hate—
> More kinds to choose from would really be great—
> That's why Azaleas's spoken here.*

The Begonia Bible

Millie and Ed Thompson recently closed their Living Museum of Begonias in Southampton, New York. With its more than 1,500 species and cultivars of begonias, operating the museum was just too
difficult. (Many of the plants were large-specimen size in containers
16 inches or larger.) Fortunately, however, for the people of New
York, the Thompsons donated their collection to the New York Botanical Garden.

Also, fortunately, during their many years of collecting and
studying begonias the Thompsons wrote a book that, many say, is
the definitive book on begonias.

Begonias: The Complete Reference Guide, by Mildred L. and
Edward J. Thompson, has over 850 illustrations—165 in full color—
and 384 pages. Features include classification of begonias, facts
and descriptive information for more than 2,450 species and cultivars, culture, special techniques, a bibliography, and more. Cover
price is $37.50, but the Thompsons are offering the book at a spe-
cial price of $25.00 postpaid. They also have a *1984 Update,* which
has 610 new entries and 301 revised entries. The price of this is
$6.75 postpaid. Order from the Thompsons, P.O. Drawer P.P.,
Southampton, NY 11968.

---

*Verse by Bob Carlson, reprinted by permission from Carlson's Gardens
1989 catalog.

Wildginger Woodlands   HARDY WILDFLOWERS,
1297 Mill Creek Run   FERNS
Webster, NY 14580
(Mailing address: P.O. Box 1091,   Mrs. Phyllis M. Farkas,
Webster, NY 14580)   Owner

Mail-order sales only; catalog $1.

Mrs. Farkas gathers seeds and plants from her home wild garden and from her 20-acre woodland in Walworth, New York.
(Because her land is rough and for insurance reasons, she doesn't
allow visitors.)

It's obvious, looking through Mrs. Farkas's catalog, that
she is a very dedicated gardener with a deep interest in wildflowers. She lists dozens of seed varieties that she has collected
and provides in-depth information on how to start them—
information that comes from her own experience.

Among many others, she had her first crop of fringed
gentian after years of trying, which included taking seedlings
along with her on most of her travels because they thrived on
a daily dip in a pond. Currently she has *Trillium grandiflorum*
and *erectum* in abundance. She stresses that all her seeds are
custom picked when *ripe*. She shares seed-starting problems and
victories with her customers.

Mrs. Farkas also lists wild ginger among her seeds.

"This," she says, "was the culprit that got me hooked on
wildflowers. Edible, if you can eat your plants. I can't."

International Bonsai Arboretum   EDUCATIONAL
1070 Martin Rd.   BONSAI SERVICES
West Henrietta, NY 14586
(Mailing address: P.O. Box 23894,
Rochester, NY 14623)   William N. Valavanis,
(716) 334-2595   Director

Arboretum open by appointment.

Take Rte. 15 south (south of Rochester); 1½ miles beyond N.Y. Thru-
way, turn left onto Martin Rd.; the arboretum is first on left.

Valavanis specializes in conducting educational bonsai courses
at his International Bonsai Arboretum, at Cornell University's
Plantations, and for bonsai and horticultural organizations
throughout the country. His annual seminars and symposia draw
people from Europe, South America, Africa, the USSR, and the
Mideast as well as the United States. More people attend these
than attend the yearly convention of the American Bonsai Society. During the rest of the year, he holds classes at the arboretum and travels worldwide, giving lectures and scouting nurseries for potential bonsai.

    Valavanis has a thorough background in his work. He
studied ornamental horticulture at the State University of New
York Agriculture and Technical College in Farmingdale and got
a B.S. degree in floriculture and ornamental horticulture from
Cornell. He filled in his background by studying bonsai and
ikebana in Japan.

    At the arboretum, classic bonsai can be viewed, studied,
and created; some 300 display-quality bonsai and several thousand bonsai-in-training are on display. The arboretum also carries a full line of supplies and plant materials for creating and
training bonsai.

    Valavanis also is the publisher and editor of *International*
Bonsai, a quarterly magazine containing bonsai advice and news.
The publication, which is beautifully illustrated, goes to sub-
scribers in the United States and forty-seven other countries.
Write for the subscription price.

Rhode Island

RHODE ISLAND

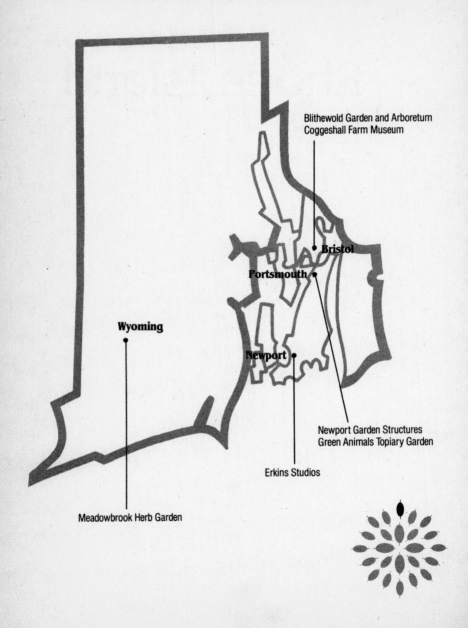

Blithewold Garden and Arboretum
Coggeshall Farm Museum

Bristol

Portsmouth

Wyoming

Newport

Newport Garden Structures
Green Animals Topiary Garden

Erkins Studios

Meadowbrook Herb Garden

Blithewold Garden and Arboretum

101 Ferry Rd. (Rte. 114)
Bristol, RI 02809
(Mailing address: P.O. Box 417, Bristol, RI 02809)
(401) 253–2707

Grounds open year-round, 10 A.M.–4 P.M.; mansion open Tues.–Sun., mid-May–Oct., 10 A.M.– 4 P.M.; closed Mon. and holidays. Admission fee; additional fee for mansion.

Between Providence, R.I., and New Bedford, Mass. Take Rte. 95 to exit 2; go south on Rte. 136 approximately 8½ miles to Griswold Ave.; take Griswold Ave. west to Rte. 114 (Ferry Rd.); go south on Ferry Rd. ³⁄₁₀ mile to arboretum.

To get a glimpse of a gracious summer life-style around the turn of the century, visit Blithewold with its 33 acres overlooking the Narragansett Bay. The forty-five-room summer home, designed along the lines of an English manor house, is bright and airy with many porches, a brick terrace, and expansive views of the gardens and bay.

Blithewold was designed by New York landscape architect John DeWolf and was originally owned by Augustus Van Winkle, a coal magnate. In the late 1970s, his daughter bequeathed Blithewold to the Heritage Foundation of Rhode Island.

The grounds include a rose garden, rock garden, and water garden. In addition, DeWolf planted numerous exotic trees and shrubs that only recently had been introduced from China and Japan. Today these are mature specimens and include Chinese cedars, ginkos, and a grove of bamboo, *Phyllostachys aureosulcata;* they average 25 to 30 feet in height and are believed to be the largest stand of bamboo in the Northeast.

A stately giant sequoia is a particularly handsome specimen. Over 82 feet tall, it has been growing approximately 1

foot per year since it was planted in 1911 and is the largest tree
of this species in eastern North America.

Brochures showing a self-guided tree tour are available,
and you'll find a gift shop in Blithewold's carriage house and
picnic areas on the grounds.

Special events include a spring bulb display in April and
a spring plant sale in May. A number of horticultural programs are offered throughout the year. Call or write for information.

Coggeshall Farm Museum
Box 562
Bristol, RI 02809
(401) 253–9062

Open Tues.–Sun., 10 A.M.–6 P.M.; winter, 10 A.M.–4 P.M.; closed
in Jan.

*In Bristol take Rte. 136 or Rte. 114 (Hope Rd.) to Poppasquash Rd.;
the museum is on Poppasquash Rd. next to Colt State Park.*

Coggeshall, on 40 acres, is an eighteenth-century working farm
restoration, featuring an organic vegetable garden with heirloom vegetables, an herb garden, a colonial orchard, and a field
of early varieties of corn and pumpkins. There are also farm
animals and a blacksmith shop. Numerous special events are
held throughout the year—maple syrup days in spring, many
craft workshops throughout the summer, and a harvest fair in
September. Call or write for information about these.

Colt State Park, adjoining the farm, has a picturesque
three-mile drive around the shoreline of Narragansett Bay and,
according to people at Coggeshall, is a "terrific place to picnic."

Erkins Studios, Inc.

GARDEN ORNAMENTS, FURNITURE,
POTTERY

662 Thames St.
Newport, RI 02840
(401) 849–2660   Ann Gerrish, Manager

Direct retail sales; open Mon., Wed., Thurs., Fri., in summer, 10 A.M.–4 P.M.; Mon., Wed., Fri., in winter, 10 A.M.–2 P.M.; other times by appointment only. Also mail-order sales; catalog and several brochures $4.

In Newport, on Thames—a one-way street; the studio is on the left-hand side; it shares a building with O'Donnells Cleaning.

Erkins Studios imports hand-carved limestone statuary, fountains, finials, and terra-cotta pots from Italy, and lead garden figures and teak garden furniture from England.

Many items can be found in the Newport shop that aren't shown in the catalog or brochures. The company goes to great lengths to locate clients' wants and will do custom work, if need be, to customers' specifications.

Although some items, as might be expected, are on the expensive side, many others are quite reasonably priced.

And, as Gerrish says, "We add the finishing touches to the loved garden."

Green Animals Topiary Garden

Cory's La.
Portsmouth, RI 02871
(Mailing address: The Preservation Society of Newport County, 118 Mill St., Newport, RI 02840)
(401) 847–1000

Open every day, May 1–Sept. 30, 10 A.M.–5 P.M.; weekends, Oct., 10 A.M.–5 P.M. Admission fee charged.

Take Rte. 114 to Cory's La.; on lane next to St. Philomena's School.

This is a fun place to take children. And it's a "must" for anyone interested in topiary. "Green animals" is what you'll see
here, almost eighty of them, sculptured from trees and shrubs.
The menagerie consists of a peacock, elephant, giraffe, cat, dog,
ostrich, lion, donkey, wild boar, swan, camel, mountain goat,
rooster, and a lot more. Also a few extras such as a policeman
and a sailboat.

Other things of interest are espaliered fruit trees, flower
beds in formal designs bordered with dwarf box, a rose garden,
a fruit and vegetable garden, even a pet cemetery surrounded
by four urns sculptured from California privet. You can also
browse through a toy museum and a gift shop where you can
buy topiary forms.

Combination tickets, at a good savings, can be purchased
for Green Animals and a number of historic homes in Newport.
Call or write the office for information.

Look! A Rhode Island Red!

Put your binoculars away. You don't look *up* to see the state bird of
Rhode Island. You look down. Rhode Island Reds, being chickens,
usually walk instead of fly.

In Rhode Island, the Rhode Island Red is taken seriously. So
seriously, in fact, that in Adamsville, Rhode Island, at the intersection of Routes 81 and 179, there's a monument to the bird. The
Red began life in Rhode Island in 1854 and that was the start of the
world's poultry industry and chicken every Sunday.

Rhode Island Reds, incidentally, lay *brown* eggs and that's
the color egg you'll find most often in markets in Rhode Island and
neighboring states. (Hint: buy them; it's best not to ask for white
eggs.)

Newport Garden Structures   GAZEBOS, OTHER GARDEN
699 Black Point Farm Rd.   STRUCTURES
Portsmouth, RI 02871
(401) 849–6850   John F. Anderson, Owner

Direct retail sales; call for appointment. Six dealers in R.I., Mass., and Conn. Brochures sent in response to inquiries. Deliveries made within 100-mile area.

Call for directions to display areas.

When Newport Garden Structures was started in 1986, it was in response to a perceived need for "high-quality" garden structures such as the Victorian era produced, says Anderson. The firm built some prototypes, set up a booth at the Boston Flower Show, and sold out a year's production capability in advance.

Gazebos of various designs are the firm's main sales items, with 40 percent of the work custom made. But it also makes bridges, arbors, benches, and other architect/homeowner-designed structures. The company uses primarily western red cedar, and to a lesser extent redwood, in construction. A limited amount of custom furniture is made of teak or painted mahogany.

Gazebos can be made in a number of sizes, and include numerous options, such as screens, fixed seating arrangements, special trims, handicapped entrances, and hot tub enclosures. Construction methods are state of the art.

The structures are handsome. And their prices, which can be around $15,000 for a top-of-the-line model, reflect their quality.

Meadowbrook Herb Garden   HERBS
Rte. 138
Wyoming, RI 02898
(401) 539–7603   Marjie Fortier, Owner

Direct retail sales; open Mon.–Sat., year-round, 9:30 A.M.–5 P.M., Sun., 1 P.M.–4 P.M. Also mail-order sales of seeds; catalog $1.

Take Rte. I-95 to exit 3A (Kingston/Newport); follow Rte. 138E for 1 mile; the garden is on right side of road.

All of Meadowbrook's herb plants (about 250 varieties) are organically grown—and have been since 1965. So you can be sure when you make a pot of herb tea or add basil to spaghetti sauce, you're not using herbs that are irradiated or fumigated.

In addition to herb plants, you can buy herb seeds, seasonings, spices, teas, and garden books—especially books on growing herbs. You'll also find organic-gardening products, botanical pesticides, compost, natural fertilizers, and herbal pet care products (such as Royal Herbal Rechargeable Flea Collars).

Meadowbrook holds frequent gardening and herb workshops. A popular special event is the annual open house held prior to Christmas, when you'll be able to sample herbal goodies, find herbal gifts, and take a special candlelight tour through the greenhouse to see the Advent Garden. Call or write Meadowbrook for specific dates and ask to be put on the garden's mailing list.

(And don't forget to buy some Royal Herbal Concentrate for recharging those Royal Herbal Rechargeable Flea Collars.)

Vermont

VERMONT

Cady's Falls Nursery

Lavoie's Green Mountain Nursery and Landscape

The Cambridge Herbary

Gardener's Supply Co.

Stone's Throw Gardens

Perennial Pleasures Nursery

Irasburg

Craftsbury

The Shelburne Museum

Cambridge

Vermont Wildflower Farm

Morrisville   **East Hardwick**

Burlington

Shelburne

St. Johnsbury Center

Charlotte

Addison Gardens
The Rock Garden

Vergennes

Bristol

Le Jardin du Gourmet

Robert Compton, Ltd.
Rocky Dale Gardens

Rathdowney

Bethel

Vermont Bean Seed Co.

Fair Haven

M. M. van Schaik

Cavendish

Mettowee Mill Nursery

Dorset

Londonderry

The Cook's Garden

Equinox Valley Nursery

The Grafton Village Nursery

Manchester   **Grafton**

Bennington   **Putney**

South Newfane

Basketville
Putney Nursery

Guilford

Bennington Potters

Floral Gates Nursery

Olallie North Daylily Gardens

Bennington Potters
324 County St.
Bennington, VT 05201
(Mailing address: P.O. Box 199,
Bennington, VT 05201)
(802) 447–7531

TERRA-COTTA POTS AND
PLANTERS

Patricia Field,
Sales Manager

Direct retail sales; open Mon.–Sat., summer months, 9:30 A.M.–8 P.M., Sun., 12 M.–5 P.M.; Mon.–Sat., winter months, 9:30 A.M.–5:30 P.M., Sun., 12 M.–5 P.M. Also mail-order sales; brochure and price list $1.

From the center of Bennington take Rte. 7 north; at the first light, turn right onto County St.; the potters yard is several hundred yards ahead on left.

For handsome, high-fired terra-cotta pots and planters a stop here should be a priority. Round, square, rectangular, fluted, round bottom, hanging, and cone shaped; classic and avant-garde designs—whatever you might want, it's here. Don't confuse these planters with ordinary clay pots; with their high firing and sturdy walls, Bennington pots should last for years. And although each planter is distinctive, it lets the plant take the spotlight. (You may have seen Bennington ware in Crate & Barrel and similar stores.)

Another plus: one room here has factory seconds where you can pick up some great buys.

Rathdowney
3 River St.
Bethel, VT 05032
(Mailing address: P.O. Box 357,
Bethel, VT 05032)
(802) 234–9928

HERBS

Louise Downey-Butler,
President

Direct retail sales; open Mon.–Sat., 9 A.M.–5 P.M., Sun., 11 A.M.–4 P.M. Also mail-order sales; write for newsletter, first issue sent free.

189

Take Rte. 89 north to Bethel exit; then take Rte. 107 west; the shop is on Rte. 107 and Rte. 12 in Bethel.

Rathdowney is a complete herbal shop where you can buy plants of ordinary and exotic herbs in spring, and seeds of herbs and wildflowers, and bulk herbs, hanging bunches of herbs, potpourri, wreaths, plant containers, and garden and craft supplies year-round.

A garden at Rathdowney sets off an 1850s federal-style building, with shop and garden overlooking the White River.

The *Rathdowney Thymes*, published four times a year, includes herbal lore, the Gardener's Corner, herb recipes, and items available by mail from the company. Rathdowney has booths at many shows and craft fairs in New England and New York throughout the year.

Robert Compton, Ltd.   SCULPTURAL FOUNTAINS,
Rte. 116   AQUARIUMS
Bristol, VT 05443
(Mailing address:
Star Route, Box 6,
Bristol, VT 05443)   Robert Compton and
(802) 453–3778   Christine Homer, Co-owners

Direct retail sales; call ahead. Also mail-order sales; color catalog $2.

Take Rte. 116, 5 miles north of Bristol; go 1 mile beyond the intersection of Rte. 17; Compton's is on the corner of Rte. 116 and Meehan Rd.

Robert Compton's water sculptures are unique, each representing hundreds of hours spent in refining form and function. The results are works of art, infusing clay with glass, water, motion, and light.

Compton's works appear in gardens, homes, and offices and have been included in many invitational shows and one-man exhibits.

He is a graduate of the University of Vermont and his wife, Christine Homer, is an art-school graduate and an avid spinner and weaver. They share a studio in what was once a cow barn.

"It is our desire to make works of art that are visually exciting," says Compton, "yet incorporate elements from nature that are soothing to the spirit. The sounds of tumbling water in our fountains and the serene movements of fish swimming in our aquariums have a calming restful effect."

Rocky Dale Gardens

62 Rocky Dale Rd.
Bristol, VT 05443
(802) 453–2782

PERENNIALS, DWARF CONIFERS

Bill Pollard and Holly Weir,
Owners

Direct retail sales only; open Wed.–Mon., Apr. 1–Dec. 1, 9 A.M.–6 P.M.; closed Tues.

About halfway between Burlington and Middlebury; 1½ miles east of Bristol at the intersection of Rte. 116 and Rte. 17; the gardens are located between two narrow concrete bridges on the south side of the road.

The 3 acres of Rocky Dale's display gardens, in island beds, have more than 600 varieties of perennials and uncommon shrubs and conifers. In back of the nursery and gardens are woods and rocky cliffs, nestled between Deer Leap and South Mountains. By walking through the gardens you can see plants as specimens and visualize how they may be used in your garden.

Among their offerings are more than thirty daylily varieties, eighteen types of astilbe, several dozen sedums, five varieties of violas, and a half-dozen varieties of thyme. The shrub and conifer collections specialize in dwarf varieties and have some striking plants.

A husband and wife team, Weir and Pollard are California transplants; Weir has a degree in horticulture and nursery management from the University of California and Pollard has a background of many years' work at a rare plant nursery and as an estate gardener. Their expertise shows in their work and is invaluable, they say, in helping and advising their customers.

Gardener's Supply Co.   GARDEN TOOLS AND EQUIPMENT
128 Intervale Rd.
Burlington, VT 05401
(802) 863–4535   Will Raap, President

Direct retail sales: open Tues.–Fri., 9 A.M.–5:30 P.M., Sat., 9 A.M.–3 P.M.; closed Sun.–Mon. Also mail-order sales; free catalog.

In Burlington take Main St. to Prospect; go north on Prospect, across intersection with Riverside Ave., bear left to Intervale Rd.

The motto of Gardener's Supply is "innovative gardening solutions," and a look around their store shows how well the company has lived up to this. Some examples:

Paperpots—biodegradable, bottomless paper pots for starting seedlings; no transplant shock when set out in garden

Windowsill Heat Tape—heating tape sized for windowsills to provide bottom heat for starting seeds

Wall O'Water—said to protect plants from temperatures as low as 10°F

Affordable Lean-To Greenhouse—assembles in minutes (priced low!)

Multi-Head Tool System—one handle with interchangeable heads is hoe, rake, cultivator, pruning saw, and weeder

Compost Aerators—simple tool for making the tough job of aerating compost simple

Earth Staples—great big staples to hold plastic mulches and covers in place

Compact Peat—small bricks of dried, pressed peat; just add water to make a gallon of peat whenever you need it

Hi-Rise Sprinkler—sprinkler head on a tripod, tall enough to reach over a corn patch

And there's much, much more. The retail store not only has the products listed in the catalogs but also many additional garden helpers.

Gardener's Supply is committed to organic gardening and has many products for extensive organic pest and weed control. As an additional help to gardeners, there are product bulletins for many items explaining the use of each in detail.

A store you're very likely to enjoy.

The Cambridge Herbary   HERBS
Cambridge Rd., Town Rd. #7
Cambridge, VT 05444
(Mailing address: R.R. 1, Box 84B,
Jeffersonville, VT 05464)
(802) 644–2480   Sally H. Bevins, Owner

Direct retail sales; open Tues.–Sun., Mother's Day weekend until last week of Aug., 8:30 A.M.–5 P.M.; closed Mon.

Cambridge is northeast of Burlington, Vt.; take Rte. 15 northeast from Winooski to Cambridge; follow state highway signs from Cambridge.

At The Cambridge Herbary you'll find over 100 different kinds of herbs, and a gift shop with dried wreaths, potpourri, herbal vinegar, books on herbs, and more. Sally Bevins has been selling herbs since 1981.

Always of interest to visitors are the forty-eight beds in Bevins's display garden, which are laid out in six concentric circles.

Mary Mattison van Schaik,   BULBS
Imported Dutch Bulbs
Tarbell Hill
R.R. 1, Box 181
Cavendish, VT 05142   Mary Mattison van Schaik,
(802) 226–7338   Owner

Direct retail sales, Sept.–Dec.; call first. Also mail-order sales, catalog $1.

Take Rte. 103 north to Rte. 131; Tarbell Hill, the location of the company, is 2 miles east of Cavendish.

Here you'll find spring flowering bulbs including tulips, daffodils, hyacinths, species and large crocus, *Eranthis, Fritillaria, Galanthus,* species iris, *Ipheion, Leucojum, Scilla,* and *Allium.* There are also many varieties of major bulbs, for example, very early species tulips, single and double early tulips, mid-flowering triumph tulips, Darwin hybrids, single late, late double, late parrot, and late lily-flowering.

You can pick up bulbs at the van Schaik warehouse in September, October, and November. However, display gardens are at their best from late April through May. Some of the bulbs planted here have been used for experimentation, but all the bulbs *sold* are imported from Holland.

Mary Mattison van Schaik, an American citizen, lived in

Holland from 1935 to 1952. During this time, she married and had six children. The business was begun in 1946, first exporting bulbs to the United States, and when Van Schaik returned to the United States with her Dutch husband and children and settled in Vermont in 1952, she began importing from Holland.

Vermont Wildflower Farm   WILDFLOWER SEEDS
Rte. 7
Charlotte, VT 05445   **Ray and Charlotte Allen,**
(802) 425–3500   **Owners**

Direct retail sales; open every day, May–mid-Oct., 10 A.M.–5 P.M. Also mail-order sales, free catalog.

On Rte. 7 between Burlington and Middlebury; 5 miles south of the Shelburne Museum.

The state of Vermont lists the Wildflower Farm as a major tourist attraction, and school tours, bus tours, and group visits bring thousands of visitors each year.

The Allens began their business in 1981 after some twenty years of interest in wildflowers and of growing wildflowers from seed. Their collection of seeds is the largest in the East so chances are they'll have what you're looking for. And all seeds have been tested in the farm's gardens.

The farm has over 6 acres of test fields and forest wildflower walks that are open to visitors. Hundreds of wildflower species are labeled and described. You can buy wildflower seeds in the garden shop where you'll also find books on growing wildflowers and wildflower-related gifts.

In July and August you can also watch a slide show of wildflowers as they appear season by season. There's a nominal admission charge in these months but children under twelve are free.

Stone's Throw Gardens

Rte. 1, Box 111
Craftsbury, VT 05826
(802) 586–2805

HARDY PERENNIALS

G. Frank Oatman, Jr., and
F. Jon Wood II, Co-Owners

Retail sales only; open Wed.–Sun., May–mid-Sept., 10 A.M.– 5 P.M.; closed Mon.–Tues.

In north central Vt.; take state Rte. 14 from Hardwick, Vt.; the signs will lead you from the turnoff from Rte. 14 at the north end of Eleago Pond to the gardens.

Stone's Throw Gardens specialize in *hardy* perennials, with hundreds of varieties. But, according to Oatman, the "deep specialties" with one of the widest selections in the Northeast are old-fashioned (heritage or shrub) roses, with about forty varieties available for sale, and true lilies (genus *Lilium*), with about sixty varieties.

"Be careful in buying roses and lilies," Oatman advises gardeners. "Both these wonderful groups contain varieties good in any location in the United States, but many of those varieties are quite specific in their requirements, especially as to cold hardiness. And many modern lilies were developed for the cut-flower market and do not hold up well in the garden. Since we are in Zone 3, our plants *must* be very cold hardy and if it does well for us it should be fine anywhere in New England! We have tried every lily and rose variety we sell and know how each performs."

An outstanding feature of Stone's Throw Gardens is simply the beauty of its setting. Display gardens extend on several levels around a restored 1795 country house, featuring perennials and roses against old stone walls, an English-style tea garden, mown walks through meadows and woods to a pond, magnificent views of Mount Mansfield and the main range of the Green Mountains, fields of colorful perennials under propagation, and a vegetable garden laid out in colonial fashion with a split-rail face. Graveled paths are linked with colorful annuals and raised beds that mix vegetable and herb rows with borders of perennials.

Not only can visitors buy plants but they can also get ideas for planting them in their own home settings.

Well worth a visit.

Mettowee Mill Nursery, Inc.
Rte. 30
Dorset, VT 05251
(Mailing address: P.O. Box 264,
Dorset, VT 05251)
(802) 325–3007

NURSERY STOCK,
LANDSCAPING SERVICES

Donna and Steve Jones,
Owners

Direct retail sales only; nursery and greenhouses open Mon.– Sat., Apr.–Nov., 8 A.M.–6 P.M., Sun., 8:30 A.M.–5 P.M.; reopens for Christmas.

Located in southwestern Vt.; take Rte. 7 to Manchester Center, then Rte. 30 north to Dorset; the nursery is about 1½ miles north of the village.

Mettowee Mill Nursery has vegetables and bedding plants in season, perennials, split-rail fencing, and trees and shrubs—many locally grown and already acclimated to local temperatures. Complete landscaping service is a major part of the business.

The nursery has experienced horticulturists on its staff and offers workshops throughout the year. Among subjects covered recently were children's gardening activities and heir-loom plant varieties—for which the nursery added four beds featuring old-fashioned annuals and perennials.

The nursery has designed unique "shrub shelters" that help protect shrubs and bushes from winter storms and snow. They look something like wooden folding ladders, are made of native spruce, are very sturdy and adjustable. For out-of-the-area gardeners these can be shipped; order by calling the nursery.

Perennial Pleasures Nursery   OLD-FASHIONED,
Brickhouse Rd.   HARDY PERENNIALS, HERBS
East Hardwick, VT 05836   Rachel Kane,
(802) 472–5512; (802) 472–5104   Proprietress

Direct retail sales only; open Tues.–Sun., May 1–Sept. 15, 9 A.M.– 5 P.M.; closed Mon.; other times by appointment.

In north central Vt.; go 2 miles north on Rte. 16 from its junction with Rte. 15 to East Hardwick; take a left leading into the village and follow the signs from Rte. 16 to the nursery; it's a brick house with a sign in front.

Dig up a copy of the September 1986 issue of *Horticulture* and read the article, on page 23, about Rachel Kane's garden. Or, better yet, visit Perennial Pleasures Nursery and talk to Kane personally. Her enthusiasm for "antique" flowers is contagious as is her general zest for gardening.

Kane got her garden basics from her father, a landscape architect, and at the University of Vermont, she had a double major—art history and plant science. When she heard a speaker who was talking about historic flower gardens mention that it was difficult to find someone who could restore these gardens or supply the flowers, Kane found her calling. That was something she would like to do. And her double majors meshed together beautifully.

Kane began gathering and growing flowers and herbs that were common in the seventeenth, eighteenth, and nineteenth centuries, and the nursery soon became a source for historic plants and information about them. Kane has supplied plants for a number of garden-restoration projects including those at the Van Cortland Manor in Tarrytown, New York, and the Rockefeller estate in Hyde Park, New York.

She now has over 500 varieties of plants at the nursery, most of which she grew from seed. Her mother, Judith, is in charge of herbs and has made a display garden for them by the barn. (She says no one has ever asked her for an herb she didn't have.)

Perennial Pleasures Bed and Breakfast

Judith Kane, Rachel's mother, also operates a bed and breakfast in the 1840 brick federal-style house at Perennial Pleasures that overlooks the village of East Hardwick and the mountains beyond. And she's in charge of the Tea Garden (she's English) where you can enjoy afternoon tea with homemade scones and whipped cream and jam, among the old-fashioned flowers.

If you're interested, call or write for a brochure on the Brick House Guests Bed and Breakfast. With its feather mattresses, handmade quilts, and an English-style "wake up" tea tray it sounds like real old-fashioned luxury.

Vermont Bean Seed Co.   VEGETABLES, HERBS,
Garden La., Box 250   FLOWERS
Fair Haven, VT 05743
(802) 265–4212   John H. Burke III, President

Direct retail sales; open Mon.–Fri., 9 A.M.–5 P.M. Also mail-order sales; free catalog.

Fair Haven is west of Rutland, Vt., on Rte. 4; the company is ½ mile south of the intersection of Rte. 4 and Rte. 22A.

Back in 1975, Vermont Bean Seed Co. started out by selling—as might be guessed—beans. The company had more than thirty-five varieties of its own bean seed. Today the bean seed inventory is said to be the world's largest, around seventy varieties, along with some 650 other vegetable, greens, herb, and flower seeds.

"We are one of the last," says Burke, "if not *the* last, of the seed industry's endangered species: a company that deals solely in the sale of untreated seeds."

The company's nonseed offerings are consistent with this theme; only biological control products are sold.

Vermont Bean Seed Co. tests all its seeds in trial gardens before they are placed on the market. Trial gardens are open to the public and, in addition, there's an All-America Selections display garden that you can visit.

The Grafton Village Nursery, Inc.   PERENNIALS
Pleasant St.
Grafton, VT 05146
(Mailing address: P.O. Box 6,
Grafton, VT 05146)   Wallace M. Brown,
(802) 843-2442   Manager

       Direct retail sales only; open Mon.–Sat., late Apr.–late Oct., 8:30 A.M.–5 P.M., Sun., 10 A.M.–12 M.; Mon.–Sat., remainder of year, 8 A.M.–4 P.M.

In southwestern Vt.; take exit 5 off I-91, then go west on Rte. 121 to Grafton; the nursery is located one block from the Old Tavern in the middle of town.

The nursery has ½ acre of well-labeled perennials (about seventy-five varieties) growing in raised beds and dug for you while you're there. Many are large-specimen plants. Two greenhouses contain a variety of flowering, hanging, foliage, and herb plants.

Specialties are vegetatively propagated geraniums (many

types and colors), Star of Bethlehem, flowering cabbage, and kale. The adjoining gift shop has a number of Vermont items, and also has a good selection of terra-cotta and handcrafted, glazed pottery.

Floral Gates Nursery   PERENNIALS
Sweet Pond Rd.
Guilford, VT 05301
(Mailing address:
R. 3, Box 305,
Guilford, VT 05301)
(802) 257–7406   Mary Filgate, Owner

Direct retail sales of plants; Mon.–Sat., May, 8 A.M.–4 P.M., closed Sun.; display gardens open Sat., June–Aug., 8 A.M.–4 P.M.; weekdays by appointment only. Admission, $2 per person; guided tours available.

In southern Vt., located at Sweet Pond State Park; take Rte. 91 from Mass. to Rte. 5 in Vt. to Guilford; at Guilford Store take a right onto Guilford Centre Rd., go 2³/₁₀ miles; then turn left onto Weatherhead Hollow Rd.; go 4¹/₂ miles; at four corners take a right onto Sweet Pond Rd.; go 2 miles to nursery/park.

The nursery has over 400 varieties of flowering perennials and shrubs. Plant sales are held in May, and the display gardens are open from June through August.

The 4 acres of display gardens slope down to a 20-acre pond and conform to the land for a natural setting. Garden markers aid in the description of sun/shade plants, and give height, color, and bloom time.

A mile-long trail, with many vistas, leads around the pond and is a bird-watchers delight. Often orioles, mourning doves, scarlet tanagers, humming birds, herons, and goldfinches, among others, are spotted.

Call ahead to arrange for a tour—available for individuals and groups.

Lavoie's Green Mountain Nursery   HARDY PLANT
and Landscape   MATERIAL (ZONE 3)
Rtes. 14 and 58
Irasburg, VT 05845   Mark Lavoie,
(802) 754–8456   Owner

Direct retail sales; open Mon.–Fri., Apr. 1–Nov. 30, 7:30 A.M.–6 P.M., Sat., 8 A.M.–5 P.M., Sun. 9 A.M.–4 P.M. Also wholesale sales.

In north central Vt.; take Rte. 91 north to Rte. 14; go west on Rte. 14; the nursery is at the corner of Rte. 14 and Rte. 58, 1 mile north of Irasburg.

The nursery has a wide selection of hardy perennials, fruit, and food-producing plants, and Lavoie is adding an increasing variety of hardy trees and shrubs. Material is northern grown and hardy to −30°F. The nursery has 60 growing acres.

Lavoie also has a comprehensive design, building, and maintenance division, which includes large tree moving. The staff consists of licensed horticulturists offering consulting services as well.

It's a no-frills, top-quality garden center, he says, for all garden needs—with an emphasis on organic fertilizers and pest controls.

The Cook's Garden   SEEDS OF SALAD GREENS,
Moffit's Bridge   HERBS, VEGETABLES
Londonderry, VT 05148
(Mailing address: P.O. Box 65,
Londonderry, VT 05148)   Shepherd and
(802) 824–3400   Ellen Ogden, Owners

Direct retail sales; May 1–Labor Day; call ahead. Also mail-order sales, catalog $1.

Take Rte. 91 north to Rte. 103 and then to Rte. 11; take Rte. 11 to Londonderry, then go ¼ mile west to Landgrove Rd.; travel 1 mile to dirt road on the right; it's ½ mile to the nursery.

Appropriately named "Looseleaf Farm," The Cook's Garden is run by Shepherd Ogden, who calls himself a "lettuce nut." Shepherd and his wife Ellen started out in the 1970s as market gardeners, selling vegetables from a roadside stand. But now they have a seed company with sales around the country.

All seeds are tested at Looseleaf Farm before going on the market. The Ogdens use organic gardening methods, selling only untreated seeds and avoiding the use of chemical insecticides or fungicides. (Shepherd's grandfather, Samuel Ogden, was an organic-gardening pioneer and author of the book *Step-by-Step to Organic Gardening*, Rodale Press, 1971.)

The Cook's Garden is definitely for salad lovers—with more than fifty varieties of lettuce, twenty chicories, seven varieties of radicchio, and herbs and vegetables (many imported), and even edible flowers.

At Looseleaf Farm, visitors are welcome during summer months when they can walk through trial plots and display gardens, and buy perennials and seeds. It's best to call ahead, however, because the Ogdens often are out in the nursery.

The Cook's Garden is also the title of a 240-page book, on which Shepherd and Ellen collaborated. It's a primer on growing all of The Cook's Garden's crops and using the garden delicacies in recipes; the book sells for $14.95 in paperback, and you can order it from The Cook's Garden or buy it from your bookseller.

Recently the Ogdens received one of the American Horticultural Society's most prestigious prizes—the G. B. Gunlogson Award—for their creativity in gardening.

Equinox Valley Nursery   PERENNIALS, NURSERY STOCK,
Historic Rte. 7A   ANNUALS, GARDEN SUPPLIES
Manchester, VT 05254
(Mailing address: P.O.B. 206,   Roger and Penny Preuss,
Manchester, VT 05254)   Owners
(802) 362–2610

Direct retail sales; open every day, Apr.–Dec., 8 A.M.–5 P.M.;
Mon.–Sat., Jan.–Mar., 9 A.M.–4 P.M. Some mail-order sales; pick up
list at nursery.

*On Historic Rte. 7A, 2 miles south of Manchester; 1 mile north of
Basketville.*

Ten years ago Roger and Penny Preuss left their landscaping
business in New Jersey and, along with their children, headed
north looking for the "better life." Their nursery started out as
an old barn and cow pasture, just about the time Manchester
was exploding from a quaint town to the "Aspen of the East."

Today they have a well-rounded retail nursery with display gardens, growing fields, eight greenhouses, and a garden
supply and gift shop. And the second generation is coming into
business with them; both their son and daughter have degrees
in horticulture.

Perennials are probably the Preusses' special interest. They
stock over 500 varieties and keep up to date by attending perennial symposia throughout the country, making contacts to
find new varieties, and getting valuable information to pass on
to their customers.

They also have bedding plants in the spring, potted annuals throughout the summer, cut flowers, and general nursery
stock. They sell fresh fruits and vegetables through the season.

One of their special events is the annual Christmas open
house held Thanksgiving weekend. You can pick out your own
fresh-cut tree or a potted live one; sip mulled cider and eat

gingerbread; and shop for Christmas plants, holly, mistletoe, and fresh balsam wreaths and garlands.

One reason for the Preusses' success may be their attitude toward customers. "We try to give people personal service," says Penny, "along with a good selection and professional help. If someone wants something we don't have, we make sure we do have it next time. We pride ourselves as being known as 'a nice place to visit.' "

Cady's Falls Nursery   PERENNIALS, DWARF CONIFERS
R.D. 3, Box 2100
Morrisville, VT 05661
(802) 888–5559   Don and Lela Avery, Owners

Direct retail sales; open Wed.–Mon., mid-April–Oct., 10 A.M.–6 P.M.; closed Tues.; call before coming in Sept. and Oct.

Take Rte. 100 north from Stowe; approximately 1 1/2 miles north of Stowe veer left onto Stagecoach Rd. at the Fox Line Inn; go about 7 miles to the end of the road; turn left and go about 1/4 mile and turn left again just before bridge; the nursery is the only place on road, about 1/2 mile ahead.

"We specialize in perennials that are hardy in zone three," says Avery. "That means thirty-five degrees below many winters. We are an old-fashioned nursery in that we grow ninety percent of what we sell and deal personally with all our customers. Our display gardens show mature specimens of many of our four hundred plus varieties of perennials. And our four acres of growing fields are open to the public and all plants are clearly marked."

Although the Averys don't sell by mail they do put out a catalog each year with descriptions of their offerings. But they ask *please* don't send for a catalog unless you plan to visit.

Don Avery adds, "The 'dwarf' conifer world is vast and

alluring and I'm afraid I'm becoming addicted in that direction. We have begun to plant specimens around the property and the new pond area seems to lend itself especially well to these graceful forms. Unlike most of the plants we offer, the conifers carry rather weighty price tags, but they are extremely long lived. And buying a small plant and watching it grow may be one of the greatest minor pleasures of the next ten years!"

The Rock Garden   HARDY PERENNIALS,
Lake Rd., Panton   HERBS, DWARF CONIFERS
Vergennes, VT 05491
(Mailing address: R.D. 3, Box 430,
Vergennes, VT 05491)   Mitzi Valentine Goward,
(802) 475–2338   Owner

Direct retail sales; also wholesale; open Sat.–Sun., 12 M.–5 P.M. or by appointment.

Located on Lake (Champlain) Rd. in Panton, ten minutes north of the Crown Point Bridge and ten minutes south of Basin Harbor Club; 7 miles from Vergennes.

"I offer quality, not quantity," says Mitzi Goward, "and specialize in some unusual plants that aren't easily found elsewhere." Some examples she mentions are *Allium senescens* 'Glaucum,' a low-mounded plant with rose pink blooms; *Filipendula hexapatala* 'Flore Pleno,' tall stems with clusters of ivory shell-like flowers; *Dianthus* 'Royal Midget,' low, neat mounds with very fragrant, tiny magenta flowers; and the dwarf pines *Pinus aristata,* a bristle cone pine, and *Pinus strobus* 'Horsford,' from a seedling originally found in Vermont.

Goward puts out a catalog listing of her plants that includes information and much helpful advice on culture. The catalog is sent without charge, but please don't ask for a copy unless you intend to visit the garden.

She also does landscaping of rock gardens and perennial beds and gives slide programs to garden groups.

Baskets and Buckets and More

If you're looking for baskets—any kind of baskets—the place to go is, fittingly, Basketville. Craftsmen in Putney, Vermont, have been making woven baskets since the early 1840s. Here, in a water-powered mill, they learned how to work with ash and oak to fashion "the best baskets that can be made."

Vermont handmade baskets are the featured items at Basketville but the company also sells other locally made woodenware plus imported rattan, willow, and wickerware products.

Among the stocks are harvest baskets, two-handled garden baskets, princess flower baskets, willow cherry baskets, wicker porch and patio furniture, wall baskets, seagrass hats for gardening, Victorian rattan fern stands, and maple sugar buckets that make great planters.

In Putney, the Basketville store (a factory outlet) is on Main St., Putney, VT 05346-0710; the phone number is (802) 387–5509. This and the stores listed below are open seven days a week, year-round, except for Thanksgiving, Christmas, and New Year's Day. Hours vary somewhat among the stores so call ahead if you want to be sure to find a store open.

Basket Barn, Inc., Historic Route 7A, Manchester, VT 05254; (802) 362–1609

Basketville of Sturbridge, Inc., Route 20, Sturbridge, MA 01566; (508) 347–3493

Basketville of Lake George, Inc., R.R. 3, Box 3205, Lake George, NY 12845; (518) 798–5504

Basketville of Cape Cod, Inc., 416 Main St. (Route 28), West Dennis, MA 02670; (508) 394–9677

There's also a mail-order division at the Putney location. For a copy of Basketville's 32-page catalog, send $1. You can call there to order, toll free outside Vermont: 1 (800) 258–4553.

Putney Nursery   WILDFLOWERS, PERENNIALS,
Rte. 5   HERBS, ALPINES
Putney, VT 05346
(Mailing address: Box 265,
Putney, VT 05346)
(802) 387–5577   C. J. Gorius, President

Direct retail sales; open Mon.–Sat., 9 A.M.–6 P.M., Sun., 10 A.M.–
5 P.M.; closed Jan., July 4, Thanksgiving, and Christmas Day. Also
mail-order sales (seeds only); catalog $1.

*Putney is in southwestern Vt.; take I-91 north to exit 4 in Vt.; the
nursery is located on Rte. 5, across from exit 4.*

Three years after graduating from Brattleboro High School, the
late George D. Aiken, former Vermont governor and U.S. senator, borrowed $100 to buy a piece of land on which to plant
some raspberries. But before he had full ownership of that land,
it had grown to 500 acres—and had become Putney Nursery.
Aiken soon was known as a pioneer in the commercial culture
of wildflowers.

At the 2-acre garden center of Putney Nursery you'll find
a very large selection of wildflowers (plants and seeds), ferns
(more than 200 varieties), perennials, herbs, and alpine plants.
All are propagated by the nursery.

The wildflower gardens, always a big attraction, are at
their best in spring and fall. A gift shop features wildflower
gifts, a large selection of clay pots, cast-iron fountains, and garden ornaments. The Christmas shop, open from late summer
on, has greens of all types, wreaths, door sprays, roping, and
the distinctively New England partridgeberry bowls.

In the gift shop you may see a copy of *Pioneering with
Wildflowers*, a classic on the subject, authored by Aiken. Be sure
to look at the book's dedication. Aiken wrote,

—to Peter Rabbit in the hopes that flattery will accomplish what traps and guns have failed to do and that the little rascal will let our plants alone from this time on.

Le Jardin du Gourmet   HERB SEEDS, PLANTS,
Memorial Drive   VEGETABLE SEEDS,
St. Johnsbury Center, VT 05863   NURSERY STOCK
(802) 748–5646   Paul Taylor, Owner

Direct retail sales; open Mon.–Sat., 9 A.M.–5 P.M.; closed Sun. Also mail-order sales; catalog 50 cents.

Take Rte. 91 (close to the Vt./N.H. state line) north to St. Johnsbury Center; Le Jardin is in town, next to Wayne Lumber.

If you read garden magazines you probably recognize the name "Le Jardin du Gourmet." You may also remember the name "Raymond Saufroy" and recall the small catalog he used to send out, jam-packed with lists of herbs and imported vegetables and recipes for using them. Saufroy, a Frenchman and former restaurant owner, says he introduced shallots (the secret of French cooking) to the United States and has sold thousands of pounds of them since.

Le Jardin continues, but Saufroy's daughter and son-in-law have taken it over. They have a nursery, greenhouse, and shop in St. Johnsbury Center and sell many of the same things Saufroy did—such as rocambole (Spanish garlic), Fraise des Bois (wild strawberries), Long d'hiver de Paris (leeks), and, of course, shallots.

You'll also find a lot of books on herbs, imported foods, houseplants, cut flowers, shrubs, fruit trees, Christmas greens in season, and much more.

It's an interesting place—especially if you're a gourmet.

🦎 The Shelburne Museum

Rte. 7
Shelburne, VT 05482
(802) 985–3344

Open every day, mid-May–mid-Oct., 9 A.M.–5 P.M. Admission
fee charged.

*Take Rte. 89 to exit 189, Shelburne; follow the signs to Rte. 7; the
museum is located on Rte. 7 in Shelburne, 7 miles south of Burlington.*

The Shelburne Museum is situated on 45 acres near Lake
Champlain and has thirty-seven period homes and historic
buildings housing a huge collection of Americana. It also has
one of the finest lilac gardens in New England plus perennial
and herb gardens.

The perennial gardens are semienclosed, surrounded by
low buildings, fieldstone walls, and hedges. They are quite formal although the plantings are simple and of a type that does
well in a northern New England climate. The herb garden has
medicinal and cooking herbs typically found in late-eighteenth-
and early nineteenth-century country gardens.

Buildings and exhibits in the museum include a circus
building, a railroad station, a steam locomotive and furnished
private railroad car, a general store, an apothecary shop, a
blacksmith shop, a round barn, and a one-room schoolhouse.
There are also several gift shops, a visitors' center, a cafeteria,
and a snack bar.

At the visitors' center you can get a list of suggested tours,
such as Life in Early New England, Early American Childlife,
or Folk Art. Because this is a large area and has much to see
besides the gardens, you'll probably want to spend the greater
part of a day here.

An outstanding event is "Festive Lilac Sunday," about the
third Sunday in May. The museum's 400 lilacs, representing
more than 90 varieties, typically reach full bloom in mid to late

May. Walking tours are conducted by horticultural experts, and a variety of exhibitors selling gardening tools, plants, and herbs will be there. Call or write the museum for the exact date.

Olallie North Daylily Gardens   DAYLILIES, SIBERIAN
Marlboro Branch Rd.   IRIS
South Newfane, VT 05351
(802) 348–6614   Christopher Darrow, Manager

Direct retail sales; open Wed.–Sun., Apr. 15–Sept. 30, 9 A.M.–5 P.M.; closed Mon.–Tues., except by appointment. Mail-order sales planned for future.

The gardens are 13 miles northwest of Brattleboro; go north on Rte. 30; turn left onto Depot Rd., then left into Williamsville; turn left again at the fork in South Newfane; it's the third house on the left. (Three lefts, third house.)

Olallie North's extensive collection of daylilies (over 500 varieties) represents thirty years of collecting by Christopher Darrow's grandfather—the late Dr. George Darrow, a plant breeder for the U.S. Department of Agriculture. Darrow and his parents moved specimens of his grandfather's entire collection to the south Vermont farm in the late 1970s and soon began to develop a daylily nursery. The name "Olallie North" came from Dr. Darrow's name for his Maryland farm, "Olallie."

The nursery covers about 4 acres with plots surrounded by grass walkways. The extensive daylily collection represents almost all daylily colors. Blooms begin in June and are at their peak in July and August; there are thousands of flowers. Some varieties bloom into late September or October, until the frost.

Plants are grown by organic methods and Darrow says he prides himself in running a nursery that carries on his grandfather's work.

Addison Gardens

R.D. 1, Box 496A
Hopkins/Fisher Rd.
Vergennes, VT 05491
(802) 759–2529

HARDY PERENNIALS

J. Paul Sokal and
Louise Giovanella, Owners

Direct retail sales; open Tues.–Sun., May & Sept., 10 A.M.–5
P.M.; closed Mon.; Tues.–Sat., July–Aug., 10 A.M.–5 P.M.; closed Sun.–
Mon. Also mail-order sales; catalog $1.

*Vergennes is on Rte. 7 and Rte. 22A between Middlebury and Bur-
lington; take Rte. 22A south from Vergennes and turn left onto Hop-
kins/Fisher Rd.; the nursery is 1½ miles, on the right side.*

Addison Gardens specializes in hardy garden plants, mainly perennials, but with some garden-scale trees and shrubs. Shade
plants are well represented among the 700 varieties.

A 2-acre rambling hillside garden displays the plants
beautifully. Many are mature specimens, which customers find
helpful in planning their gardens and in visualizing the end
effect. The informality of the gardens, Sokal says, appeals to
them.

Sokal and Giovanella are inveterate collectors and have
many unusual plants that aren't for sale. "It's not so much that
we wouldn't sell them," Sokal says, "but there isn't much call
for things such as two-inch *Thalictrum* (meadow rue) or the six
or seven *Asarum* (wild ginger) cultivars we grow."

The
Gardener's
Calendar

Mark your calendar now. Here are annual events taking place in the gardening world throughout the year. Specific dates, of course, vary from year to year, but the *approximate* time is indicated. Following each listing is a phone number that you can call to get exact dates and times.

Many events are listed as "early," "mid," or "late" within each month. To make sure you don't miss them, call well in advance.

JANUARY

Late January, Camellia Days and Camellia Sale, Lyman Estate, Waltham, Massachusetts; (617) 891–7095

Late January, Annual Camellia Show, Arnold Arboretum, Jamaica Plain, Massachusetts; (617) 524–1718

FEBRUARY

Mid-February, "Winterbloom" and Plant Sale, Bartlett Arboretum, Stamford, Connecticut; (203) 322–6971

Late February–early March, Hartford Flower Show, Civic Center, Hartford, Connecticut; (203) 529–2133

Late February–early March, Boston Flower Show (oldest flower show in the country), Boston, Massachusetts; (617) 536–9280

MARCH

Early March, Annual Worcester Spring Flower Show, The Centrum, Worcester, Massachusetts; (508) 869–6111

Early March, Greenhouse Plant Sale, Lyman Estate, Waltham, Massachusetts; (617) 891–7095

Mid-March, New York Flower Show, New York, New York; (212) 757–0915

APRIL

Early April, Annual Spring Plant Sale, New England Chapter of American Gloxinia and Gesneriad Society, Waltham Field Station, Waltham, Massachusetts; (617) 891–0650

Early April, Annual Vermont Maple Festival, St. Albans, Vermont; (802) 524–5800

Mid-April, Greater New York Orchid Show, New York Botanic Garden, Bronx, New York; (212) 220–8700

Last weekend in April, Daffodil Show, Berkshire Garden Center, Stockbridge, Massachusetts; (413) 298–3926

MAY

First Wednesday and Thursday in May, Plant Sales, Brooklyn Botanic Garden, Brooklyn, New York; (718) 622–4433

Early May, Plant Sale, Fuller Gardens, North Hampton, New Hampshire; (603) 964–5414

Early May, Annual Dogwood Festival, Greenfield Hill, Fairfield, Connecticut; (203) 259–0573

Early May, Spring Plant Sale, Blithewold Garden, Bristol, Rhode Island; (401) 253–2707

Mid-May, Rhododendron Flower Show and Auction, Massachusetts Chapter of American Rhododendron Society, University of Massachusetts Suburban Experiment Station, Waltham, Massachusetts; (617) 891–0650

Mid-May (ten days), Lilac Festival, Highland Botanical Gardens, Rochester, New York; (716) 244–8079

Mid-May, Plant Sale, Bartlett Arboretum, Stamford, Connecticut; (203) 322–6971

Mid-May, Plant Fair and Sale, Berkshire Garden Center, Stockbridge, Massachusetts; (413) 298–3926

Mid-May, Lilac Sunday, Arnold Arboretum, Jamaica Plain, Massachusetts; (617) 524–1718

JUNE

Mid-June, New England Wild Flower Society's Annual Plant Sale, Garden in the Woods, Framingham, Massachusetts; (617) 237–4924 or (617) 877–7630

Mid-June, New England Gardening Day, Strawberry Banke, Portsmouth, New Hampshire; (603) 433–1100

Mid-June, Herb Fair, Berkshire Garden Center, Stockbridge, Massachusetts; (413) 298–3926

Late June, Rose Sunday, Sonnenberg Gardens, Canandaigua, New York; (716) 394–4922

Late June, Open House, Lowe's Roses, Nashua, New Hampshire; (603) 888–2214

JULY

Mid-July, Annual Open House/Garden Days, Camden, Maine; (207) 236–4404

Late July, Annual Connecticut Agricultural Fair, Goshen Fairgrounds, Goshen, Connecticut; (203) 379–2527 or (203) 633–7550

AUGUST

Early August, Annual Candlelight Tour, Historic Houses and Gardens, Strawberry Banke, Portsmouth, New Hampshire; (603) 433–1100

Early August, Garden Days, Old Sturbridge Village, Sturbridge, Massachusetts; (508) 347–3362

Early August, Maine State Fair, Bangor, Maine; (207) 947–3542

Early August, Annual Open House and Field Day, Comstock, Ferre & Co., Wethersfield, Connecticut; (203) 529–3319

Mid-August, Flower Show, Berkshire Garden Center, Stockbridge, Massachusetts; (413) 298–3926

Late August, New York State Fair, Syracuse, New York; (315) 487–7711

SEPTEMBER

Early September, Vermont State Fair, Rutland, Vermont; (802) 755–5200

Early September, Annual Woodstock Fair, South Woodstock, Connecticut; (203) 928–2346

Early September, Annual Goshen Fair, Goshen, Connecticut; (203) 491–3604

Fall Foliage Time

Mid-September to mid-October, Vermont and New Hampshire
Fall Foliage Hotlines: Vermont, (802) 828–3249; New Hampshire, (603) 244–2525

Mid-September, Common Ground County Fair, Maine Organic Farmers and Gardeners Association, P.O.B. 2176, Augusta, Maine; (207) 622–3318

Mid-September (twelve days), Eastern States Exposition, West Springfield, Massachusetts (one of largest county fairs east of the Mississippi); (413) 737–BIG E

Late September, Fall Open House, Betsy Williams/The Proper Season, Andover, Massachusetts; (508) 475–2540

Late September, Chrysanthemum Festival, Bristol, Connecticut; (203) 589–4111

Late September, Annual Fall Flower Show, Planting Fields Arboretum, Oyster Bay, New York; (516) 922–9201

Late September, Annual Plant Sale and Auction, Arnold Arboretum, held at Case Estates, Weston, Massachusetts; (617) 524–1718

OCTOBER

First weekend, Annual Nineteenth-Century Agricultural Fair, Genesee Country Museum, Mumford, New York; (716) 538–6822

First Saturday, Harvest Festival, Berkshire Garden Center, Stockbridge, Massachusetts; (413) 298–3926

NOVEMBER

First Tuesday (election day), Annual Plant Sale, Brooklyn Botanic Garden, Brooklyn, New York; (718) 622–4433

Thanksgiving Day through the following Sunday, Open House, Ludlow Herb Farm, Ludlow, Massachusetts; (413) 598–9875

DECEMBER

Early December, Annual Christmas Open House, Meadowbrook Herb Garden, Wyoming, Rhode Island; (401) 539–7603

Early December, Annual Christmas Plant Sale, Lyman Estate, Waltham, Massachusetts; (617) 891–7095

The Medalists:
The All-America Winners

See the Best New Flowers and Vegetables

If you're starting vegetables or flowers from seed, you can depend on those whose packets carry the red and blue logo, "All-America Selections Winner." For over fifty years the nonprofit All-America Selections (AAS) organization has been rating vegetables and flowers, using uniform standards, and testing them in trial gardens throughout the country. The best each year are named AAS winners.

You may not always agree that these choices are the *very* best—but they are seeds that should thrive in your garden.

At the many AAS display gardens throughout New England and New York you can see recent flower and vegetable winners. And this may help you decide what to grow next year.

Here are the AAS display gardens listed by state.

Connecticut
4-H Farm Resource Center, Simsbury Rd. (Rte. 185), Bloomfield, CT 06002

Maine
Ornamental Trial Gardens, University of Maine, Rangely Rd., Orono, ME 04469

Massachusetts
University of Massachusetts, Durfee Conservatory, French Hall, Amherst, MA 01003

Berkshire Garden Center, Inc., Rte. 102, Stockbridge, MA 01262

New Hampshire
University of New Hampshire, Prescott Park, Portsmouth, NH 03801

Fuller Gardens, 10 Willow Ave., North Hampton, NH 03862

New York
Cutler Botanic Gardens, 840 Front St., Binghamton, NY 13905

Brooklyn Botanic Garden, 1000 Washington Ave., Brooklyn, NY 11225

Arboretum of Greater Buffalo, Forest Lawn Cemetery, 1411 Delaware, Buffalo, NY 14209

Cooperative Extension, Erie County Botanical Garden, South Park and McKinley Rds., Buffalo, NY 14218

Sonnenberg Gardens, 151 Charlotte St., Canandaigua, NY 14424

Queens Botanical Garden Society, Inc., 45–50 Main St., Flushing, NY 11355

Holtsville Ecology Site, 249 Buckley Rd., Holtsville, NY 11742

Wild Winds Farms, Hunts Hollow Road, Naples, NY 14512

Mohonk Mountain House, Mountain Rest Road, New Paltz, NY 12561

Liz Christy Garden, Bowery and Houston Sts., New York, NY 10012

Nassau County Cooperative Extension, 1425 Old Country Rd., Plainview, NY 11803

Sterling Forest Gardens, Tuxedo, NY 10987

Rhode Island
Blithewold Gardens and Arboretum, 101 Ferry Rd., Bristol, RI 02809

University of Rhode Island, Plant Science Department, Kingston, RI 02881

Green Animals Topiary Garden, 380 Cory's La., Portsmouth, RI 02871

Vermont
Vermont Bean Seed Co., Route 22A, Fair Haven, VT 05743

University of Vermont Extension Service, Horticultural Research Center, Rte. 7 South, South Burlington, VT 05401

All-America Rose Selections

A reliable guide to a quality rose bush is a small green-and-white tag on it that says AARS or All-America Rose Selections.

Each year roses are submitted for testing at some two dozen trial gardens throughout the country. After a two-year period, the best, according to official judges, receive the coveted green-and-white tag. Competition is tough and usually less than 4 percent of the roses tested receive the award.

As plant patents last only seventeen years, an AARS rose, after seventeen years, can no longer wear the tag. But it's still a great rose and many remain in commerce. One of the best-known roses ever introduced—'Peace'—was an AARS in 1946 and can be found today at many nurseries.

Preview Next Year's Winners at AARS Public Rose Gardens

To see next year's AARS winners before they're offered for sale, visit one of the following public rose gardens. Winners for the coming year are officially announced each June and they will be growing and marked in AARS gardens in your area. This will also give you a good chance to see how they're performing in your climate.

AARS Public Rose Gardens

Connecticut
Norwich Memorial Garden, 200 Rockwell Street, Norwich

Elizabeth Park Garden, 160 Walbridge Road, West Hartford

Maine
Deering Oaks Park Rose Circle, 227 Park Avenue, Portland

Massachusetts
James P. Kelleher Garden, Park Drive, Boston
Stanley Park of Westfield, 400 Western Avenue, Westfield

New Hampshire
Fuller Gardens, 10 Willow Avenue, North Hampton

New York
Edwin deTurk Bechtel Memorial Garden, New York Botanical Garden, Bronx
Cranford Memorial Garden, Brooklyn Botanic Gardens, Brooklyn
Joan Fuzak Memorial Garden, Erie Basin Marina, Erie Street, Buffalo
Sonnenberg Gardens, 151 Charlotte Street, Canandaigua
Queens Botanical Garden, 43–50 Main Street, Flushing
United Nations Garden, New York
Old Westbury Gardens, Old Westbury Road, Old Westbury
Central Park Garden, Wright Avenue and Central Parkway, Schenectady
Dr. E. M. Mills Memorial Garden, Thomdon Park, Syracuse

Networking with Other Gardeners

Get in touch with other gardeners. Join them in meetings, go on tour together, share the latest gardening news, take part in workshops, plan flower shows . . . the list could go on and on.

Three states have large horticultural societies that offer a smorgasbord of activities for members. Check into the following; even if you're not a resident of the state, you're welcome.

The Connecticut Horticultural Society
150 Main St.
Wethersfield, CT 06109
(203) 529–8713

A year's membership in the Connecticut Horticultural Society includes monthly lectures by experts; spring flower show tours; spring garden tour of several days; hands-on workshops; Saturday garden visits to special gardens; monthly newsletter, with information, growing tips, and news; and library privileges.

Massachusetts Horticultural Society (MHS)
Horticultural Hall
300 Massachusetts Ave.
Boston, MA 02115
(617) 536–9280

A year's membership includes a bimonthly publication, *The Leaflet,* with current news about the society, a calendar of coming events, articles on culture, and news from the plant world; a year's subscription to the monthly garden publication, *Horticulture;* tours, workshops, and classes; complimentary tickets to the annual Boston Flower Show; a plant hot line to call when you have plant problems; and borrowing privileges at the MHS Library (the oldest horticultural library in the United States and also one of the largest), which includes borrowing and returning books by mail.

The Horticultural Society of New York (HSNY)

128 W. 58th St.
New York, NY 10019
(212) 757–0915

Basic yearly membership includes subscription to society publication; listings of all educational programs; discounts on educational programs, books, and plants in the HSNY greenhouse shop as well as discounts from many participating floral shops and gardens in the area; on-site library use; plant line call-in service and walk-in horticultural advice; free members' annual gift plant; and participation in members-only previews and events. "Full Membership" and "Sustained Membership" have many additional benefits.

The Specialty Plant Societies

Joining one of these societies is a sure way to find other gardeners who share your plant likes and problems. Here are some of the plant societies in the New England and New York area, many of which have chapters in these states.

In almost all cases no address is given. The societies change officers frequently and it's difficult to keep a list up to date. To find out who you should contact for membership information, try the following: (1) check with nurseries or growers who specialize in your particular plant, (2) check with one of the three state horticultural societies, or (3) check recent gardening magazines.

American Begonia Society
American Bonsai Society
American Camellia Society
American Dahlia Society, Inc.
American Fern Society
American Gloxinia and Gesneriad Society
American Hemerocallis Society
American Iris Society
American Ivy Society
American Penstemon Society
American Peony Society
American Rhododendron Society
American Rock Garden Society
American Rose Society, P.O.B. 3000, Shreveport, LA 71130
Gesneriad Society International
Herb Society of America
Hobby Greenhouse Association
Ikebana International
Indoor Gardening Society of America, Inc.
International Lilac Society, Inc.
New England Bromeliad Society
North American Gladiolus Council
Northeast Bonsai Association
Saintpaulia International

The New England Wild Flower Society

Since 1922 the New England Wild Flower Society has been promoting conservation of native plants—through research and education in botany, horticulture, and ecology. The society has active state chapters throughout New England.

At the Garden in the Woods, the society's 45-acre botanic garden, more than 1,500 varieties of native plants are grown and new propagation techniques are tested. People are encouraged to grow wildflowers at home by using the plants and seeds made available by the society.

Membership includes a quarterly newsletter, educational programs at reduced rates, free admission to the Garden in the Woods (see pages 74–75), borrowing privileges at the society's library, and discounts on plants and books. Call or write the society for more information on membership: The New England Wild Flower Society, Hemenway Rd., Framingham, MA 01701; (617) 237–4924.

Protecting Nature Throughout the World— The Nature Conservancy

Whether it involves prairie orchids in Illinois, whooping cranes in Nebraska, the short-beaked baldrush in New York, the spotted wintergreen in Vermont, or endangered ferns in Rhode Island, the Nature Conservancy is taking action. Not only does it have conservation projects in all fifty states, but also in Canada, Latin America, and the Caribbean.

If you would like to get involved too, contact one of the following offices of the Nature Conservancy:

Connecticut Chapter, 55 High St., Middletown, CT 06457; (203) 344–0716

Maine Chapter, 122 Main St., Topsham, ME 04086; (207) 729–5181

Massachusetts/Rhode Island Field Office, 294 Washington St., Rm. 740, Boston, MA 02108; (617) 423–2545

New Hampshire Field Office, 7 S. State St., Suite 1, Concord, NH 03301; (603) 224–5853

New York Field Office, 1736 Western Ave., Albany, NY 12203; (518) 869–6959

Vermont Field Office, 138 Main St., Montpelier, VT
05602; (802) 229–4425

Conserving the Massachusetts Landscape

For almost 100 years an organization called The Trustees of
Reservations (TTOR) has been acquiring and preserving land
of scenic, historical, or ecological value throughout Massachusetts. These are properties that were threatened by development, neglect, pollution, and so on that the organization has
either purchased outright or received as gifts.

The Trustees of Reservations was established in 1891 by
Charles Eliot, a young landscape architect who later became a
partner of America's dean of landscape architects, Frederick Law
Olmsted.

To date TTOR owns and manages more than seventy
reservations totaling over 17,500 acres. It also protects an additional 6,000 acres.

Reserves include well-known places such as Bartholomew's Cobble and Naumkeag and other less-known areas such
as Misery Islands Reservation, an 84-acre deserted island in Salem
Bay that you can only reach with a private boat after getting a
boat pass from the U.S. Geological Survey. And because these
properties are saved for the people, the public is encouraged to
enjoy them.

The trustees have published a guidebook to the properties that describes each in detail and also lists the various activities permitted—such as nature study, bird walks, canoeing, cross-
country skiing, hiking, and swimming. In addition, there are
many special events such as horticulture lectures, plant sales,
canoe trips, and even concerts. The guidebook, *A Guide to Properties of The Trustees of Reservations,* is $3 from TTOR, 572 Essex
St., Beverly, MA 01915; (508) 921–1944.

The TTOR welcomes members, who receive a number

of special benefits. If you're interested call or write at the address and phone number above for information.

Give the Birds a Hand

One of the world's oldest conservation groups—which, in fact, came into existence less than thirty years after the word "ecology" joined the English language—is the Audubon Society.

The name was the idea of George Bird Grinnell, who used it in 1886 in honor of his late friend and mentor, John James Audubon. Within a few years societies were organized in Massachusetts and Pennsylvania.

Thanks in part to Rachel Carson's *Silent Spring*, the infamous DDT is now a poison of the past, the Audubon Society is flourishing, and over seven million Americans are maintaining plantings specifically to provide food and shelter for birds.

If you're not a member of the Audubon Society, why not join and give the environment a helping hand. Here's where you can get information in New York and New England:

Audubon Council of Connecticut
Rte. 4, R.R. 1
Box 171
Sharon, CT 06069
(203) 435–2004

Maine Audubon Society
Gilsland Farm
118 Rte. 1
Falmouth, ME 04105
(207) 781–2330

Massachusetts Audubon Society
South Great Rd.
Lincoln, MA 01773
(617) 259–9500

Audubon Society of New Hampshire
3 Silk Farm Rd.
P.O.B. 528B
Concord, NH 03301
(603) 224–9909

National Audubon Society
950 Third Ave.
New York, NY 10022
(212) 832–3200

Audubon Society of Rhode Island
40 Bowen St.
Providence, RI 02903
(401) 521–1670

The Massachusetts Audubon Society owns and protects over 18,000 acres of land in the commonwealth and has lists of various sanctuaries. Contact the other states for information about their areas.

Birds in Your Backyard*

If you'd like birds in your backyard, these are the four keys to attracting them: adequate (1) food, (2) water, (3) shelter, and (4) nest sites.

*Information above is from the brochure, "Birds in Your Backyard," prepared by the Massachusetts Audubon Society and the Massachusetts Nurserymen's Association.

Plant trees and shrubs that will give the birds the seeds and fruit they need throughout the year and you'll also be providing shelter and nest sites. (For birds that want hole nesting—chickadees, swallows, and wrens—you can put up simple nest boxes.) The following are some plants suitable for home landscapes that will do well in the Northeast.

Fruit-bearing plants (preferred by robins, bluebirds, thrashers, wrens, starlings, finches, and more):

American holly (*Ilex opaca*)—bright red berries

Allegheny shadbush (*Amelanchier laevis*)—small tree with edible fruit

Black adler (*Viburnum molle*)—blue-black fruit in fall

Bunchberry (*Cornus canadensis*)—red berries

Checkerberry or wintergreen (*Gaultheria procumbens*)—red berries

Cranberry cotoneaster (*Cotoneaster apiculatus*)—large red berries

Dwarf American cranberry bush (*Viburnum americanum compactum*)—scarlet fruit

Highbush blueberry (*Vaccinium corymbosum*)—edible berries in summer

Northern bayberry (*Myrica pennsylvanica*)—waxy gray berries

Partridgeberry (*Maitchella repens*)—small shrub with red berries

Winterberry, female (*Ilex verticillata*)—bright red berries in fall

White rugosa rose (*Rosa rugosa alba*)—white flowers all summer, large red hips

Seed-bearing plants (favorites of goldfinch, sparrow, chickadee, blue jay, grackle, song sparrow, cardinal, nuthatch, and more):

Blue fescue (*Festuca ovina* var. *glauca*)—a grass with edible seeds

Canoe birch (*Betula papyifera*)—abundant seeds in winter

Dwarf mugo pine (*Pinus mugo* var. *pumilio*)—low, slow growing, dark green needles

Dwarf Norway spruce (*Picea abies* var. *maxwelli*)—short, bright green needles

Upright white pine (*Pinus strobus* var. *fastigiata*)—long needles

You might also consider planting a wildflower garden in a corner of your yard, with seed-producing flowers such as black-eyed Susans, goldenrod, thistles, and evening primroses.

Help Is
Close By

Abe Lincoln and Agriculture

Lincoln is not generally associated with agriculture, but agriculture, horticulture, and the many related fields got off to a healthy start during his presidency.

On May 15, 1862, the U.S. Department of Agriculture (USDA) was established. And less than two months later, on July 7, 1862, the Land Grant Act was approved.

The Land Grant Act began with a Vermonter, Senator Justin Smith Morrill of Strafford. In 1862 he persuaded his colleagues in Congress to turn over public lands in several states so they could start public colleges to "teach agriculture and the mechanic arts." This eventually led to the establishment of state university systems throughout the country.

The University of Vermont, in Burlington, which was chartered in 1791 as a private institution, added a land-grant college in 1865.

The other land grant universities in the Northeast came into existence after the Land Grant Act and include

University of Massachusetts, Amherst, 1863

Cornell University, Ithaca (New York), 1865

University of Maine, Orono, 1865

University of New Hampshire, Durham, 1866

University of Connecticut, Storrs, 1881

University of Rhode Island, Kingston, 1892

Help Is as Close as Your Telephone

The leaves on your azaleas are turning brown and you don't know what's wrong. You want to plant a few dwarf apple trees and need some advice on best varieties. When is it safe to set out tender plants in the spring?

Just get on your phone and ask your county Cooperative Extension Service (CES). To locate your local office, check the telephone listings under county government headings (it might be listed as "Agricultural Extension Service").

The CES is a joint venture of the USDA and each state land grant university. Its purpose is to further horticulture and agriculture within each state and to bring help down to the local level.

You'll find local CES offices in almost every county in New England and New York. Offices are usually staffed by one or more graduate horticulturists, often assisted by "Master Gardeners." The latter are experienced gardeners who have completed forty hours of intensive instruction in horticulture and who volunteer their services to aid other gardeners.

If the people at the CES can't answer your questions or help you in other ways, they usually will be able to refer you to a source that can. (And if you're interested in becoming a Master Gardener, call your CES office for information.)

New Vegetables from the Land Grants

Some concrete—maybe edible is a better word—proof of the value of university research is the following. It's a list of vegetables named All-America winners in recent years, the result of university breeding programs. All are still popular with home gardeners.

Bush Acorn Squash 'Table King'—University of Connecticut, 1974

Corn 'Golden Beauty'—University of Massachusetts, 1955

Lettuce 'Buttercrunch'—Cornell University, 1963

Squash 'Waltham Butternut'—University of Massachusetts, 1970

Watermelon 'New Hampshire Midget'—University of New Hampshire, 1951

The watermelon 'New Hampshire Midget' received a special Gold Medal award for representing a major breakthrough.

John Scarchuk, a former professor of horticulture at the University of Connecticut, introduced the squash 'Table King,' and after his retirement continued plant breeding. He is responsible for a number of All-America Selections awards and has the rare distinction of receiving awards for both vegetables and flowers (ornamentals).

The Cornell Peat-Lite Mix

Most gardeners, at one time or another, have used a "soilless" mix, and for this they owe much to researchers at Cornell. Back in the 1960s, James W. Boodley and Raymond Sheldrake, Jr., did a great deal of work with soilless mixes and produced material for a booklet published by the Cornell Extension Service: *Cornell Peat-Lite Mixes for Commercial Plant Growing.*

Today most commercial growers use some variation of this mix and it served as the starting point for the many mixes now sold in garden centers and nurseries—such as "Jiffy Mix," "Pro-Mix," and "Grow Mix."

It's simple and economical, albeit a little dusty, to mix your own. Here's a tested version:

    8 gallons of vermiculite
    8 gallons of shredded sphagnum peat moss
    4 tablespoons of ground limestone
    1 tablespoon of powdered superphosphate
    8–16 teaspoons of 5–10–5 fertilizer

You can put the works in a sturdy plastic garbage bag and mix it up well by tipping the bag upside down and right side up repeatedly. Be sure to moisten the mix thoroughly while it's still in the plastic bag. This will save you money if you have some large planters to fill.

If you'd like to read the Cornell booklet send $1 to Distribution Center C, 7 Research Park, Cornell University, Ithaca, NY 14850. As for *Cornell Peat-Lite Mixes*, code 1411B–43.

Plant an Heirloom Vegetable Garden

The Department of Vegetable Crops at Cornell has put together a collection of seeds representing typical varieties of vegetables grown in the nineteenth-century gardens of the Northeast.

This is an interesting project and you'll have an opportunity to observe advances made in vegetable varieties and also compare tastes and appearances with produce of the 1990s.

Vegetables include tasty yellow fingerling potatoes, tennis ball lettuce—considered one of the most delicious lettuces of all times, and tiny tomatoes, commonly called "love apples," which were considered poisonous in early years and grown as ornamentals.

For a brochure about the Heirloom Project write to Heirloom Vegetable Garden Project, Roger A. Kline, Department of Vegetable Crops, Plant Science Bldg., Cornell University, Ithaca, NY 14853-0327. A 30-page booklet describing all the vegetables and their uses is $3 (ask for bulletin 177, *The Heirloom Vegetable Garden*).

Every year during the first weekend in October, the Genesee Country Museum in Mumford, New York, holds their Nineteenth-Century Agricultural Fair at which all growers of heirloom gardeners are invited to exhibit. The museum is located on Flint Hill Rd., Mumford, NY 14511; (716) 538–6822.

Plant Hardiness Zones

One of the most familiar publications of the Department of Agriculture (USDA) is the "Plant Hardiness Zone Map," which is reprinted in hundreds of books and catalogs. Unfortunately, the large USDA map, showing subzones on one side and that used to be available for 25 cents from the superintendent of documents, is out of print. The National Arboretum (3501 New York Ave. N.E., Washington, DC 20002), working with horticulturists and gardeners throughout the country, is updating and improving the former USDA map and it should be available in the near future.

Another plant hardiness zone map in wide use is the one prepared by the Arnold Arboretum. As its zones vary somewhat from the USDA zones, you should check which map is being used when a plant's hardiness is rated. *Wyman's Gardening Encyclopedia* and the catalog of the White Flower Farm both use the Arnold map. (To get a copy of the "Arnold Arboretum Plant Hardiness Zone Map" send $1.50 to the Publications Office, Arnold Arboretum, 15 Arborway, Jamaica Plain, MA 02130–2795.)

The Meterological Evaluation Services (MES) has published another set of zone maps based on evaluation of temperature data reported by more than 200 National Weather Service Stations around the country. These maps plus a report on weather findings are $4.95 from the MES, 165 Broadway, Amityville, NY 11701.

All of this should help you choose the right plants for your area. Just be prepared for that one winter in ten, or twenty, or fifty when temperature drops to a record low—and protect all those plants that are of marginal hardiness.

~ Index